Rachel Storm is a freelance journalist and author. She has written the book *The Search for Heaven on Earth* (Bloomsbury) about the New Age movement, and specializes in work on cults and the paranormal.

RACHEL STORM

EXORCISTS

The Terrifying Truth

Fount
An Imprint of HarperCollinsPublishers

Fount Paperbacks is an imprint of
HarperCollins*Religious*
Part of HarperCollins*Publishers*
77–85 Fulham Palace Road, London W6 8JB

First published in Great Britain
in 1993 by Fount Paperbacks

1 3 5 7 9 10 8 6 4 2

A catalogue record for this book is
available from the British Library

ISBN 0 00 627653-9

Printed and bound in Great Britain by
Cox & Wyman Ltd, Reading, Berkshire

Contents

Introduction

This is a book filled with strange, chilling and even terrifying tales: tales more suited, it would seem, to some Gothic horror story than to twentieth-century life. And yet, if we are to believe the characters who relate these tales, each one of us in our everyday life is under constant threat from evil forces personified as demons and the devil. These malevolent creatures are, we are told, determined to insinuate themselves into our bodies, our minds and our souls and turn our lives into a living hell. They can condemn us to seemingly endless depressions or they can, through their relentlessly malevolent presence, drive us to suicide or murder.

But this is not simply a book about evil presences. Rather, it focuses on the lives and work of those people who devote their time to overcoming evil through the ritual of exorcism. These days, many exorcists prefer to call the ritual deliverance, but its aim is the same: that is, to bind the evil force and so free the person under its influence. For the most part, I have focused on the work of exorcists within the Christian Church. The majority of religions, however, have their demons and demon-slayers.

Since the beginning of time, thousands of millions of people from all walks of life and from a variety of spiritual backgrounds have unwaveringly believed in the very real existence of evil presences. Not surprisingly, when writing this book, the most frequent question I was asked was whether or not I was one of them: did I believe in demons?

It is a point on which I can make no final judgment. One line of argument holds that if the exorcists and the possessed individuals I spoke to were genuine, then the demons must be real.

So, were the people I spoke to genuine or were they deliberate frauds?

Most certainly, throughout history 'fake exorcists' have made their appearance. Some seem to have been in the business either for money or power and to have consciously faked their 'cures' with the help of the allegedly possessed individual. Likewise, there have been those who have deliberately faked possession in order to gain a certain degree of recognition, or acquire a certain cachet within their community.

Another possibility is that demonic phenomena do indeed make their appearance in ways which as yet defy our normal understanding of the world. They could, for instance, be the result of such influences as telepathy and telekinesis – a possibility we shall look at in chapter five.

A further possibility is that the evil presences are real only in the minds of the exorcists and possessed individuals. In this situation, it might be said that the demons are real to all intents and purposes, but it still does not answer the question of whether or not the demons have any external reality.

For instance, the possessed individual might unconsciously give a demonic shape to the darker side of their nature – maybe after having read horror stories or seen horror movies. Certainly, the more demons are talked about, the more they seem to appear and at some religious meetings, under the influence of a powerful preacher, a form of almost mass hysteria can persuade those under the preacher's spell to see such creatures.

In such a situation it is easy to see how the exorcist might succeed in the task of deliverance simply because of his or her shared belief in the root of the possessed individual's problem.

There are, of course, permutations of the above instances such as a fraudulent exorcist successfully exorcizing an unconsciously fraudulent possessed individual in order to bring them peace of mind.

Still, this does not answer the question of whether or not demons are real. Fraud – unconscious or otherwise – might explain some cases. But to reduce demons to a real versus nonreal debate is missing the point. In the realm of the spiritual – some would say in all realms – reality is only relative. The question of genuine versus fake is irrelevant. Believers certainly believe demons to be real and by far the majority of people I spoke to were, in my opinion, genuine believers, unfailingly truthful in their accounts of their experiences.

At the end of the day, it is up to the reader to judge whether or not the characters encountered in this book are genuine, or taking part in some massive, macabre hoax. On occasion, I have allowed my opinion of the people I spoke to to show through but for the most part I have held back from commenting on their testimonies and have simply allowed them to speak for themselves.

As far as this book is concerned, far more pertinent than the question of whether or not demons are real is why, in the late twentieth century, exorcism is a boom industry. That is something which this book looks into.

Yet it must not be forgotten that, although possession

and exorcism can be looked at from a sociological or psychological perspective, there are stranger things in heaven and earth than we have ever dreamed of. Although some 'demons' may be explained away, this by no means refutes their existence.

1

The Show Begins

As the credits roll up the screen, the terrified audience sit as if impaled to their seats. Since *The Exorcist*'s release in 1973, a new generation of cinemagoers has grown up. But the film still holds its old magic: the power to generate an almost debilitating fear.

The story of *The Exorcist* is simple enough: an innocent young girl, Regan, is possessed by a demon. Her mother, puzzled by the child's untoward behaviour, escorts her round a series of the country's top psychiatrists. The professionals draw a blank. Finally, despite her antipathy towards religion, the mother calls in a couple of Jesuit priests who exorcize the girl. Regan recovers. The priests die gruesome, technicolour deaths.

But what was it that so horrified – and continues to horrify – the film's audiences? Was it simply the spectacularly detailed special effects, the most notorious being the lingering shot of Regan's head revolving 360 degrees? Or was it something more? The horror film was not a genre new to the 1970s, and there have been far more graphic and gruesome films since. Yet something made a small knot of even the most hardened horror-film addicts steer clear of *The Exorcist*. There was, they felt, something inherently evil about the film, something which might possibly rub off on them. American evangelist Billy Graham was not alone in believing there was an evil power embodied in the very celluloid itself.

Even the film-makers began to feel more than a little uneasy as the list of mishaps and tragedies that occurred during the film's shooting grew longer and longer. Within the first week of filming *The Exorcist*, the grandfather of child star Linda Blair, who played Regan, died, as did the brother of Max von Sydow, the actor who played the part of Jesuit priest Father Ryan. The sense that something was out there, jinxing the cast, grew stronger as one after another suffered accidents. Even the sceptics were forced to think again when Irish actor Jack McGowran died only a week after he had completed the filming of his death scene – a horrifying end at the hands of the demon.

Still, there were those who said that the rumours were simply another promotional gizmo, a ploy which helped to make *The Exorcist* the highest grossing film ever made up to that time, with initial box-office takings in excess of £66 million. And for director William Friedkin, the mysterious series of events provided a convenient and colourful excuse for the film's having fallen behind schedule. Sceptics were, however, quick to point out that accidents and deaths were bound to occur over the period of a year, the time it took to shoot *The Exorcist*. None the less, the tales held sufficient threat for at least one person to turn down the offer of work on *Exorcist III*, a follow-up film released in 1990.

William Peter Blatty, author of the best-selling book on which *The Exorcist* was based and scriptwriter of the film, was also plagued by modern-day myth-making and rumour. He was, so the story went, a sinister, brooding and demonic individual who held elaborate Satanist ceremonies in the basement of his house in Aspen, Colorado. His wife, too, was assigned a role in the ever-more-fevered tales of terror.

She had, allegedly, given birth to a child with no eyes who turned out to be none other than the Devil.

Just as fantastic rumours surrounded the film of *The Exorcist*, so gory embellishments tend to insinuate themselves into accounts of real-life exorcisms. For all its gloriously sensational special effects, *The Exorcist* was said to be modelled on a real-life case. Was this 'real case' no more than the product of over-fevered imaginations, too? In an area where the truth is often stranger than fiction, the facts are hard to pin down. According to those who steadfastly refuse to believe in the world of supernatural powers, exorcism is simply an area where those with over-vivid imaginations can let off steam. But wherever so-called 'objective' truth lies, these ghoulish accounts of devils and demons tell us some fundamental truths about men and women's view of themselves in relation to the universe.

Prior to *The Exorcist*, Blatty was known, if at all, as a comedy scriptwriter. His interest in the dark side of life was stirred when he heard of a case of alleged demonic possession and exorcism which occurred in 1949. Blatty intended to write a factual account of the incident, but the exorcist concerned was refused permission to speak out by his bishop who was anxious to protect the privacy of the family concerned.

Despite this setback, Blatty was determined to make use of what information he had and so modelled *The Exorcist* on the case – that of Douglass Deen who lived with his family at number 3210 Bunker Hill Road, Washington. The boy was in his early teens when he allegedly became possessed by the Devil. To begin with, he began to leave a trail of strange phenomena in his wake: objects were thrown about, his mattress slid across the floor when he was asleep, the armchair he was sitting in would tilt over at alarming angles, pictures moved and a strange scratching sound came from the walls.

Eventually the boy was taken to Georgetown University Hospital where he shouted and cursed in Latin, a language he had never studied. When the medical staff found they were unable to help him, Catholic priest Father Albert Hughes was called in to conduct an exorcism. Douglass was held to the bed with leather straps but managed to burst one of the bonds. With his free hand he pulled out a bedspring and attacked the priest, tearing open his arm. None the less, the priest persisted with the ritual, noticing to his surprise that unusual scratch marks appeared and disappeared on the boy's body and that he spoke in a strange language.

The exorcism was not a success. Apparently, Father Hughes became introspective and smiled less following the event. He only once discussed his experiences of the exorcism at any length. A few days later, he died.

The Deen family then turned for help to a Jesuit priest from St Louis, Missouri. Having gained permission from his bishop, the priest conducted numerous exorcisms over a period of several weeks. During the exorcisms, the boy would scream, curse and shout in Latin. At long last, the exorcisms had the desired effect and the boy was free of the so-called possessing entity. Afterwards, he had no recollection of what had happened to him.

The residents of Bunker Hill Road believe their neighbourhood is still paying the price for the devilish goings-on of 1949. The number of horrific murders in the area is, they say, unusual in the extreme; and they claim the number of natural deaths is extraordinary, too.

Just as the real-life case on which *The Exorcist* was modelled has been blamed for numerous crimes and deaths, so too has the film. The press were determined to make the most of the by now attention-grabbing exorcist tag. 'Boy dies after seeing *The Exorcist*' ran one newspaper headline in 1974. (1)

The story suggested that the terrifying film had triggered off a fit in the sixteen-year-old Londoner, who had been suffering from something akin to epilepsy for several years. A verdict of death from natural causes was recorded and the coroner, summing up, said simply: 'If there is a moral from this tragedy it is not so much that you shouldn't go to frightening films but that if you are taking treatment for epilepsy you should continue it.' (2)

Some offenders themselves claimed their atrocities had been inspired by the film. In one case a twenty-four-year-old man from North Wales re-enacted a scene from *The Exorcist* with an eleven-year-old girl three hours after seeing the film. The man, convicted for indecent assault, said he had been 'disturbed and upset' by the film. Passing sentence, the judge said: 'A major cause in what you have done has been the influence of a particular kind of horror film where sex and violence are portrayed, especially a film called *The Exorcist*.'

The most chilling case was that of a teenage boy from Yorkshire who savagely killed a nine-year-old girl. The killer told police that he had been possessed by evil after seeing *The Exorcist*. He had, he claimed, begun dabbling in black magic and experimenting with a ouija board. Before long, he continued, he began to have nightmares about Satan and Mendoss, Prince of Darkness, and soon found that he started to feel 'mean and nasty towards people' and to enjoy mutilating and killing small birds. Referring to how he came to kill the little girl, he said:

'It was not really me that did it, you know. There was something inside me. I want to see a priest. It is ever since I saw that film, *The Exorcist*. I felt something take possession of me. It has been in me ever since.' He finished by saying, 'She stopped twitching and I knew she was dead. That is all I can say, except I am sorry. I think that inside it wasn't really me that was doing this terrible thing.'

Are such claims simply an attempt on the part of the person in question to evade personal responsibility for their actions? Psychiatric opinion tends to suggest that while film audiences may indeed be influenced by what they see on screen, it is difficult to pinpoint a process of precise cause and effect in their ensuing behaviour. None the less, the little girl's killer was not alone in believing himself to be possessed after watching *The Exorcist*.

Jesuit priest, Father John Tracy, had already steeled himself for the onslaught. Years later he recalled: 'When the film *The Exorcist* came out, I said to my companions here: "Heavens, we're in for it now. We're going to be inundated with people who think they're possessed." I had six in the first week.'

Anglican clergyman Canon John Pearce Higgins was worried not just about the psychological effects of the film, but also about its potential spiritual harm. 'Unless protest [about *The Exorcist*] from the Church is successful, we shall have a crop of schizophrenics with us soon – and a small number of cases of genuine possession,' he told *The Guardian* in 1974.

The Reverend Trevor Dearing holds *The Exorcist* responsible for sending his way at least some of those people who thronged through the doors of his church in the early seventies. He believes that many, having seen the film, were inspired simply by fear to seek him out. He also believes, however, that through the film, 'people began to learn about the symptoms of demon possession, and would start to shout and believe they had become possessed. They would produce demonic symptoms, but were really only in a state of hysteria.' (3)

Before long, the Reverend Dearing found himself transformed into a media celebrity. Tall and well-built, dressed in checked, flared trousers and with his long hair reaching down to brush below the neckline of his purple jumper, he was an eye-catching figure even to those ignorant of his calling in life. Add to his appearance the fact that he was an Anglican clergyman and the Reverend Dearing began to radiate even more of a presence. But it was his ministry of exorcism that had the tabloid journalists falling over one another to have him emblazoned across their front pages.

He was 'Trendy Trev'; he was 'The Mod Minister'. Above all else he was 'The Exorcist Vicar'. But the Reverend Dearing was far from being simply a media fabrication. In a very real sense, he was – and is – the person whose ministry marks the beginning of the twentieth-century revival of exorcism in the Christian Church within Britain.

It was in the early 1970s that the Reverend Dearing was making front-page news. But his ministry of exorcism did not come out of the blue. Instead, it was bound up with his long search for a deep and living spirituality. Trevor's story begins some forty years before his run-in with the media, in the town of Hull on the north-east coast of England.

★　★　★

A sickly child both physically and emotionally, Trevor describes his childhood as having been a 'living hell', fraught with nightmares, strange fears and imaginings. When he was well enough to attend school, he would choose to sit by the classroom door in order to ensure he could make a quick escape if overcome by a panic attack. He never quite knew what he was trying to escape from. All he knew was that he was frightened of everything, including life itself.

According to a psychiatrist who attempted to sort out the teenage Trevor, he was suffering from intense hysteria, anxiety neurosis, chronic depression, suicidal tendencies and symptoms of paranoia. Among his physical disabilities were asthma, bronchitis, arthritis and curvature of the spine. Most specialists considered him a hopeless case. But then it was not the specialists who were to set him on the road to recovery. It was in a cavernous Methodist meeting hall in Hull that Trevor first discovered Christianity. For the first time in his nineteen years, he felt that life just might hold some promise. Gradually he experienced a build-up of confidence, a spreading sensation of peace – and his spine began slowly but surely to straighten out.

Such was the impact of Christianity on his life that, despite feeling inadequate, Trevor longed to spread its message far and wide. The necessary encouragement came when someone suggested he become a Methodist preacher. His training began at Cliff College in Derbyshire and was followed by a stint as the lay pastor of a Methodist circuit in Norfolk. In order to become a minister, he then studied at Wesley Theological Methodist College in Leeds. Here the emphasis was on academic study rather than evangelistic fervour – and Trevor emerged at the other end with a

Divinity degree under his belt but considerably less fire in his heart.

None the less, he still had enough fervour to be saddened by the spirit-breaking grind of the Methodist circuit he was appointed to in Yorkshire. Most of his time seemed to be spent in committee meetings rather than in preaching. And besides, as a circuit minister who constantly had to travel from church to church, he felt unable to develop anything more than a superficial relationship with those he preached to.

After two years, Trevor resigned, having already decided that the Church of England might provide the deeper spirituality he was looking for. There followed more study, this time at an Anglican college in Birmingham. Once again, he emerged with a head full of facts which he attempted to put to good use first as a curate, then as the vicar of three Anglican churches in Yorkshire. Again, however, he felt that the true essence of Christianity was missing. He had been wrong, he decided, in thinking it could be found in a different denomination. Now he was convinced that it was missing from the Church as a whole. What should have been a vibrant, dynamic body of Bible-believing people was instead a dead, rather stuffy and superficial set-up where the so-called 'churchgoers' were more interested in the details for the next cheese and wine party than in developing their spirituality.

The time had come for another change of direction. This time, Trevor took up a religious education teaching post at a school in Essex. The experience proved desperately disheartening. After two years of classroom grind, Trevor was almost at the end of his tether, desperate to cling on to his Christianity but beginning to lose hope that he would ever find a fulfilling form of worship and ministry. It was at that point, when he had all but hit rock bottom, that he discovered the gifts of the Holy Spirit.

Trevor's wife, Anne, a nurse whom he had met at a Cliff College conference, had attended a meeting held by a travelling evangelist, Peter Scothern. She had returned home full of amazing tales of people suddenly walking after being wheelchair-bound for years, of others being delivered from evil spirits, of a deaf man suddenly hearing again – of miracle after miracle. Trevor was sceptical. Along with many Anglicans, he had been taught that the miraculous power of the Holy Spirit evident in biblical times remained firmly in the past.

These gifts are referred to by St Paul in 1 Corinthians 12:

> But the manifestation of the Spirit is given to every man to profit withal. For to one is given by the Spirit the word of wisdom; to another the word of knowledge by the same Spirit; To another faith by the same Spirit; to another the gifts of healing by the same Spirit; To another the working of miracles; to another prophecy; to another discerning of spirits; to another divers kinds of tongues; to another the interpretation of tongues; But all these worketh that one and the selfsame Spirit, dividing to every man severally as he will.

Through his theological training, Trevor had come to feel that, in the modern world, belief in such phenomena amounted to little more than ignorant superstition. He could see that divine healing and deliverance might certainly have been appropriate in the early Church as a means of explaining medical conditions which were not then scientifically understood. But he reasoned that in this day and age, with our supposedly superior knowledge of the workings of the human mind, it was the duty of Christians to reinterpret the demons of Scripture in terms of psychological disturbances.

None the less, intrigued, Trevor attended one of Scothern's meetings. It began with the preacher supposedly casting an evil spirit out of a young man. Trevor was taken aback. But before long he was feeling tremendously excited: all around him he was seeing concrete evidence of the power of the Holy Spirit. At the end of the meeting Scothern called on members of the congregation to come forward and be baptized in the Holy Spirit. Trevor was not one of those who rushed to the front of the meeting hall. He still felt a little uncomfortable with this naked display of emotion. And besides, he wanted to look into the phenomenon of the Holy Spirit a little more closely before committing himself.

So it was that in 1969, Trevor stumbled across the Charismatic Renewal Movement which was beginning to take off worldwide. The emphasis for charismatics is on an intensely personal experience of God's power, not only internally but also externally through manifestations of the gifts of the Holy Spirit. According to the 1981 official report, *The Charismatic Movement in the Church of England*, the rise of the charismatic movement was simultaneous with that of the sixties counterculture. Certainly, followers of both longed for direct personal experience of what might be termed altered states of consciousness and strove to become one with some intensely powerful life-force – whether God or some less precisely defined concept of Love and Peace. The emphasis was on intuition and spontaneity – or, putting it another way, of 'letting it all hang out'.

After looking into this new and rapidly growing movement, Trevor finally received his baptism in the Spirit. The experience was disappointing. Later, however, when he was praying by himself in his home, he suddenly broke into tongues. It was, he says, like being 'lost in rapture, ecstasy and bliss'. According to many Christians, speaking in tongues is just one living proof, which others can witness, of the power of the Spirit. For those not accustomed to the gift, it can be slightly alarming to witness: suddenly someone will start speaking what sounds like gobbledegook but is officially known as *glossolalia*, an ecstatic wordless utterance which is attributed to God. When the gift was first given to Jesus's disciples at Pentecost, some of the witnesses were amazed. Others mocked and said the disciples must be drunk. For the disciples, however, the gift of tongues was proof that Jesus was still very much alive and working amongst them. And this is precisely the promise the gifts of the Holy Spirit hold for twentieth-century charismatics. For many, the experience of speaking in tongues is the first step towards a totally new experience of spirituality, of a form of Christianity which emphasizes the supernatural power of God.

Certainly, after speaking in tongues, Trevor experienced a sensation of being filled with a new power: he felt endlessly blessed, suffused with energy and truly reborn. In the gifts of the Holy Spirit, he had finally found what he had been looking for – living, breathing evidence of God's supernatural power.

But if God's supernatural power had been rediscovered, so, too, had the Devil's.

Writing in 1970, the charismatic Anglican Michael Harper, now Canon of Chichester Cathedral, claimed:

'We are living at a time of expanding supernaturalism, good and bad. On the one hand there is the charismatic revival . . . on the other hand, there is the resurgence of the power of evil supernaturalism on a truly daunting scale.' (4)

Or as Trevor put it: 'The Baptism of the Holy Spirit not only opens one's eyes to the reality and experience of the supernatural endowment of the Holy Spirit in His miraculous abilities, but also to the reality of those 'principalities and powers, spiritual hosts of wickedness in high places' of which St Paul speaks in Ephesians 6, and, of vital importance, the victory of Christ over them.'

Like most charismatics, Trevor believes the Church is engaged in spiritual warfare, and that it is a war which few of the denominational churches are aware of:

'Human beings want peace and happiness and yet there seems to be a force or power which is forever working against our wellbeing,' he says. 'It is a war which the charismatic movement emphasizes and has insight into.'

Indeed, many charismatics believe that they have been specially chosen by God to don the armour of Christ and engage in battle against the powers of darkness. According to David Watson:

For the spiritual conflict with Satan, God too recruits and trains his own fighting forces: Christians make up the army of the Lord on earth. In the heavenly realms, he deploys legions of angels and archangels, of cherubim and seraphim. In this world, he primarily uses men and women specially picked and prepared. They are people

who have been reborn spiritually, made partakers of divine
life, and endowed by the Holy Spirit with particular
individual abilities to serve Christ's cause. (5)

Trevor readily admits that the idea that Christians are
permanently engaged in battle against the powers of evil
can be taken to extremes. He cites the example of a group
of charismatic Christians who thought their prayers were
being hindered by a woman who was wearing a blouse with
a small dragon embroidered on one of its lapels. In
Revelations, the Devil is portrayed as a dragon and so they
made her take her blouse off and burn it. 'There are
excesses,' Trevor admits. 'But spiritual warfare is very, very
real today.'

Soon after his baptism in the Spirit, Trevor left his
teaching job and went back into parochial work. In 1970
he was appointed vicar of St Paul's Church in Hainault,
Essex. It was there that he says he was first pushed into battle
with evil spirits. It was a battle for which he soon proved
to be particularly well-equipped.

But nothing in what Trevor describes as his 'very liberal'
theological training had prepared him for what he now
found himself up against. Until becoming a charismatic, he
had stood by the widely accepted Christian view that the
discoveries of modern medicine had done away with New
Testament demons. He had happily taken the line that
demons were in fact no more than a primitive people's
explanation for matters they failed to understand. As one
theologian, writing in the 1950s, put it: 'No one can use
the electric light and the radio or the discoveries of modern
medicine and at the same time believe in the New
Testament world of spirits and miracles.' (6)

Trevor's introduction to the reality of God's supernatural power had, however, also opened his eyes to the reality of evil. He could no longer accept that the New Testament teaching about demons was simply an interpretation of what today would be called an illness or emotional condition. Something far more real, and far more terrifying, was at large.

It was with a huge sigh of relief that Trevor swept the cobwebs of academe from his head and instead turned to the New Testament for confirmation of his new-found belief in supernatural powers. From its pages, he concluded that anyone who refused to believe in demons and the Devil was discrediting the ministry of Jesus:

'You can't read the New Testament without being involved in the possibility of someone having demons,' he says. 'And if you don't believe in the authority of the Christian ministry to expel demons, you do damage to the essence of New Testament teaching. If Jesus was wrong about spiritual reality, where can he be trusted?' Having become a charismatic, it was all suddenly quite straightforward: 'I believe demons exist because I take the New Testament seriously and am a very devout Christian,' Trevor explains.

One of the first cases of demonization Trevor claims to have encountered was that of Marina, a teacher who believed she had been cursed. For two years Marina suffered appalling nightmares and hallucinations, and eventually turned for help to two Pentecostal ministers. When, in the middle of exorcizing her, Marina attempted to strangle them, the ministers gave up and she ended up in psychiatric care.

Eventually, Marina found her way to St Paul's. Trevor

immediately sensed her trouble and began to pray for the woman. As with her first exorcism, Marina's response was to make a beeline for Trevor's throat. Confident in the power of Jesus, however, Trevor persisted and after only ten minutes the so-called evil spirit appeared to depart.

'I had been given no training at theological college in this type of ministry,' says Trevor, 'but I knew instantly what to do. My mind flashed back to instances of exorcism in the New Testament and I simply copied them.'

Over the years, Trevor claims to have cast out well over a thousand demons. Faced with people claiming to be possessed or breaking out into fits of rage in the middle of one of his church services, he has simply trusted in God's power and done what seems appropriate. Learning from experience, he has come to the conclusion that the most effective form of exorcism is simply to tell the evil spirit possessing the troubled individual to depart in the name of Jesus. There is no need, he insists, for pyrotechnics, special words or rituals. Instead, what is absolutely necessary is the exorcist's unshakable faith in God's supreme power.

According to Trevor, if somebody genuinely wants to become a different person and wants to go a different way in their lives, their deliverance will be effective.

'I don't believe they require all-night exorcisms or high-flown language. It is very important just to talk and find out the problem, to offer some wise counsel and then to minister in the name of Jesus Christ and tell all the evil spirits to go out of the person's life. If the person is sincere, there's no need for a prolonged ministry.' He adds, however, that the person must genuinely repent the sins they have committed, renounce them and believe implicitly in Jesus's power to deliver them. They must also, he says, continue in the Christian faith.

Word of Trevor's special abilities soon spread and St Paul's began to act as a magnet to all those who felt troubled by evil spirits. Some, says Trevor, were drug addicts, others prostitutes, others witches. But they all felt that they were possessed by some powerful evil entity which only the stronger power of Jesus could overcome. At first they came only from the London area, but as Trevor's reputation spread, so too did his ministry.

'At St Paul's, I wasn't casting spirits out of mature Christians but out of people with huge problems in their lives and from very confused backgrounds. The charismatic scene embraces the down-and-outs. Our ministry drew people whose lives had gone horribly wrong. We felt for the first time that we were really doing some positive good for people.'

One of the problems confronting all exorcists is the need to ensure that the troubled individual really is in need of deliverance rather than, for instance, simply counselling. For Trevor, one means of finding out whether the person is demonized is to delve into their past. If they have, for instance, been drug addicts, witches or prostitutes he is almost certain that their activities have opened them up to invasion by demons. Trevor also believes that people with psychic abilities are in need of deliverance, as are those who indulge in what he describes as 'perverted sexual behaviour such as homosexuality'. After delivering homosexuals, Trevor will give them healing ministry and will advise them to try hormone therapy, or 'whatever else can strengthen one kind of sexuality or another'.

He recalls one occasion when his proffered ministry of

deliverance was rejected by two women who, he says, destroyed the life of the Midlands church they were associated with by screaming, shaking and generally causing havoc during services. According to Trevor, the women's lesbian relationship was the cause of the unrest. 'The pastor was in terrible trouble. In the end, he was so worn out that he had to seek psychiatric help.' Trevor solved the problem by advising the pastor to tell the women to leave the church. He did so, and order was restored.

Other people Trevor immediately recognizes as possessed are those who react violently to the name of Jesus or are unable to take Communion. Once, a service at St Paul's was interrupted by a young man who began to howl, as Trevor describes it, 'like a werewolf'. His teeth were bared and he ran backwards and forwards like a caged animal. Trevor was horrified but none the less confronted the man and commanded the evil spirits to leave him in the name of Jesus. Almost instantly, the man fell to the floor and then jumped to his feet praising God. Trevor was just as astonished as the congregation. But he soon became accustomed to the apparent power of Jesus's name.

Another means of discovering whether someone is possessed is by the gift of discernment of spirits which is mentioned along with the other gifts of the Holy Spirit in 1 Corinthians 12. Trevor believes that he himself has this gift and is thereby enabled as it were to 'sniff out' evil spirits. 'It's rather like feeling someone come into a room without looking round,' he explains.

For Christians, there is no arguing with God-given gifts and this makes the area extremely tricky to deal with. How can it be ensured that those who really have the gift of discernment are not simply deluding themselves

– or, worse, deliberately deluding others? There is no easy answer.

Some Christians embellish the New Testament promise of the gift of discernment and say that it is a gift of 'discernment-exorcism', although no gift of exorcism is mentioned in the Bible. They justify their claim by saying that, since exorcism always followed discernment in the New Testament, the two are inextricably linked and that the Apostle Paul, author of Corinthians, must have expected people to make the connection. Clearly, it is an area where people can get carried away.

The untoward happenings at St Paul's inevitably drew attention, not only from the press but also from other Anglican clergy.

'In those days many people considered me an extremist,' says Trevor. 'Several members of the clergy called for my resignation. Anglican vicars regarded me with great suspicion – mainly because of the exorcisms I was conducting. Exorcism was considered with a very bad odour – as sensationalist and dangerous – and I was practising it publicly. Some bishops wouldn't allow me to conduct services in their dioceses.'

None the less, for five whole years, the church of St Paul was besieged by hundreds of people seeking help – more often than not, in the form of deliverance. In 1975, Trevor left St Paul's. He and his wife, Anne, now have their own itinerant ministry. They conduct about fifty missions a year all over Britain and also counsel people in their Lincolnshire home.

To meet Trevor today, it is hard to picture him as the headline-grabbing vicar of yesteryear. He still is an imposing figure, and perhaps betrays a love of show in the several decorative rings which adorn his fingers. But what is most striking is his concern that the ministry of exorcism should be balanced by common sense.

Since leaving St Paul's, Trevor has carried out fewer exorcisms, although not, he insists, because demand has waned. Rather, it is because he finds the ministry of exorcism tremendously emotionally demanding. But if someone starts manifesting symptoms of possession during one of his mission meetings – for instance, by calling out 'Jesus is dead, I saw him die' – Trevor will deliver the person immediately.

He recalls one recent meeting when he encountered a young woman who suddenly collapsed onto the floor and began crying, throwing herself about and screaming. Trevor managed to establish that she heard voices telling her to commit suicide but that she was frightened of death. He prayed for her and commanded the evil spirits to depart, whereupon she began to shake all over before, just as suddenly, recovering.

'These days I perform hit-and-run raids,' says Trevor. 'Because we are always travelling from place to place ministering to people there is no chance of checking on a person's background or counselling them before we deliver them. We simply have to deal with the problem as it arises.' Afterwards, however, Trevor will leave the person he has delivered in the hands of local Christians for follow-up care. The young woman mentioned above is now being counselled by two people from her local church.

Today, the sensational 'Exorcist Vicar' of yesteryear might be considered very middle-of-the-road. Not that he has toned down his ministry. Rather, the excesses of other Christians, whom we shall encounter in later chapters, have endowed him with a glow of respectability. Trevor is, for instance, critical of those exorcists who treat all psychological illnesses as problems with demons.

'Manic depression is often treated as if it is a demon whereas it's a chemical imbalance and can be treated with medication,' he says. 'Manic behaviour can often take on a religious tone and can be looked upon as a demon whereas I look on it as an emotional manifestation of a chemical abnormality.' In his opinion, 'Those Christians who exorcize people for virtually any problem in their lives can be extremely dangerous.'

These days, when ministers ask Trevor for advice on how to conduct exorcisms he tells them simply, 'Keep it short. If the exorcism is not immediately effective, disengage from the ministry and start counselling the person.' If the person Trevor ministers to needs more than just a short deliverance, he begins to suspect that the problem is not demonic. In such cases, he believes the trouble is likely to have stemmed from the individual's psychological or emotional problems.

Trevor does not, however, go to the other extreme which takes the line that deliverance works purely through the power of autosuggestion.

'Some people today will recognize that people are helped by the ministry of deliverance but they will say that these people find relief purely through the emotional atmosphere generated at charismatic meetings and during the deliverance itself,' he explains. 'They say that using the name of Jesus with authority and using the power of suggestion can produce a beneficial result in the person without having to posit the existence of an entity called a demon.'

Despite not holding this view, Trevor is occasionally

persuaded to put its line of thinking into practice. One such case was that of a young man who contacted Trevor at his home and begged to be exorcized. The man was, says Trevor, troubled by having paid £1000 to visit a prostitute and was obsessed with the idea that his problem was demonic. He insisted on throwing himself against walls, attempted to hurt himself in all manner of ways and claimed to be repeatedly spun round physically by some force beyond himself. In Trevor's opinion, however, the man was emotionally sick. Nevertheless, he ministered deliverance to him thinking that it might at least be of some psychological help to him. He was not happy with the result: the man was very shaky and Trevor's son came in to find him rolling around on the grass at the bottom of the garden. Trevor advised the man to seek psychological help but was unable to ensure he did so.

According to Trevor, 'The deliverance ministry is a real need for a few, but their number is far outweighed by the many people who need healing emotionally.' He estimates that three out of four cases he encounters result from non-demonic problems. While some of the cases of alleged demonic possession he has come across turn out to stem from emotional problems, others prove to be cases where a person deliberately fakes possession as a means of drawing attention to him or herself. With the help of God, and his own hard-won experience, Trevor is generally able to distinguish between the two, he claims.

He recalls being asked to visit a church in Cornwall. The pastor of the church was attempting to deal with a woman from whom he had already allegedly cast out more than a hundred and fifty evil spirits. None the less, the woman claimed that she was still in need of further exorcisms. By the time the pastor spoke to Trevor, he was so exhausted he had almost reached the end of his tether. Moreover, because he was devoting so much time to the woman, his church was in disarray. Trevor met the woman and, he says, immediately sensed she was no more than a massive attention seeker.

'She had already been through two or three churches and they had decided they could do nothing more for her. In my opinion, she was deeply emotionally disturbed but until she faced her real problems, she would not get any better. You can't carry on casting out demons for ever. If a person does have several demons, then they will almost always come out all at once when they are exorcized, not one at a time. In the New Testament the ministry of deliverance is very quick, effective and permanent – no matter how many demons are involved. I believe people who are involved in casting out all manner of demons are involved in hysterical manifestations.'

The case of Derry Mainwaring Knight provides a chilling example of how someone might fake possession not simply as an attention-seeking ploy but as a money-making venture. In the late 1980s, Knight claimed that he was possessed by Satan and that he needed thousands of pounds with which to buy regalia in order to defeat the Devil. Numerous Christians stumped up the cash.

The Knight case points up the possibility of becoming obsessed by the battle against evil to the point where any vestige of common sense disappears. It is an obsession with evil which is becoming increasingly apparent as we approach the end of the twentieth century.

In Trevor's opinion, many unthinking and naive people and ministers are these days overstepping New Testament teaching on deliverance. 'They are simply getting carried away by their enthusiasm about the reality of demons and the devil,' he says. 'The charismatic movement emphasizes the reality of much biblical teaching but today many people seem to view that as a licence for going way beyond New Testament teaching and reading all sorts of nonsense into it.' He is extremely dubious about the approach towards deliverance taken by some of today's exorcists, and points to their use of such ritualistic accoutrements as salt and water during their ministry. None the less, Trevor thinks Britain is currently witnessing an increasing need for the ministry of exorcism.

'As the teaching of Christ slackens in the country I feel the spiritual warfare intensifies, that the forces of darkness get stronger and are given more inroads into our society. This country was once protected by the fundamental Christian faith which it heard and practised. Since the advent of nineteenth- and twentieth-century liberalism, since the Church began to destroy belief in its own faith in the Bible, evil has made inroads. The Devil hasn't had to do a lot of harm in the Church because the Church has done it for itself.'

The Exorcist, arriving as it did with the onset of the seventies, was right for its time. For many people washed up on the tide of the sixties, God seemed very, very far away. According to Trevor, 'People were, and still are, fed up with formal Christian worship where God does nothing and doesn't seem to be alive.' The old saying that the Devil has all the best tunes holds more than a little truth. The portrayal of evil in *The Exorcist* might be terrifying, but at least it was real. It inspired a concrete, tangible emotion – fear. But fear was better than nothing, better than emptiness, which for many was all the mainstream Churches seemed to offer.

Christians have time and again cited *The Exorcist* as a catalyst for the late twentieth-century upsurge in Satanism. As Peter Anderson writes in his book *Satan's Snare*: 'Films such as *Rosemary's Baby, The Exorcist* and Steve Spielberg's *The Poltergeist* have all come out of the broom closet and have made demonology respectable and entertaining.' (7)

William Peter Blatty, the author of *The Exorcist*, was, however, bemused by most of the controversy surrounding the film. After all, he said, he was on the side of the good guys. Indeed, though the two Jesuit priests die carrying out the final exorcism on Regan, they do overcome the demon.

When the inevitable follow-up to *The Exorcist* was released in 1977, the film at first achieved poor box-office takings. Apparently, the cinema-going public disliked the first version of the sequel they were treated to because good was seen unashamedly to triumph, at which point they threw things at the screen. According to *Exorcist II*'s director John Boorman, the idea that good should win through was an 'unpopular' and 'unrealistic' notion. As a result, the film had to be completely re-edited. This time, although the Devil was not allowed entirely to rule the roost, neither was he vanquished.

The triumph of evil was clearly something people could believe in and relate to.

In a moving few lines at the end of *The Exorcist*, after Regan has been rid of the demon, a friend of the two dead priests asks her mother, 'What do you think really happened? . . . as a nonbeliever. Do you think she was really possessed?'

Regan's mother replies 'Well, like you say . . . as far as God goes, I am a nonbeliever. Still am. But when it comes

to a devil – well, that's something else. I could buy that.
I do, in fact. I do . . . the Devil keeps advertising, Father.
The Devil does lots of commercials.'

The priest looks at her, then says quietly, 'But if all of
the evil in the world makes you think that there might be
a Devil, then how do you account for all the good in the
world?'

'That's a point,' replies Regan's mother.

It is a point, however, which is notoriously difficult to
grasp.

2

The Devil Finds Work

Regan's mother was not alone in finding it easier to believe in Satan than in God. Satan got results. And that's what the children of the sixties wanted. The 1960s was a decade when people sought direct experiences, some through hallucinatory drugs or a variety of alternative therapies – others through the promise of Satanism. It was a decade of experimentation, of rebellion and of the breaking of taboos.

Many opted out of the Christian worldview altogether by turning to newly formed cults or Eastern religions. Others sought a deliberate reversal of Christianity. Their rebellion was to worship not God but the Devil, to seek not after good but after evil – to become, that is, Satanists.

Satanism is, according to countless Christian experts on the subject, an expressway to becoming possessed by demons or the Devil. Most Christians argue that those who choose to worship Satan are asking the Devil to enter their lives: in other words, they are deliberately asking to become possessed by Satan and so, in the eyes of Christians, are in dire need of being exorcized. But if Satanism is a reversal of Christianity, it is interesting to look at one or two Satanist groups: in doing so, a good deal can be deduced about the impression Christianity makes on those who choose to turn their backs on it.

The Church of Satan was founded by Anton LaVey in San Francisco in 1966. It is the largest movement of modern

Satanism and gathered an international following. LaVey attracted, and played up to, huge media attention, helped by the fact that film director Roman Polanski hired him to play the part of Satan in his 1968 film *Rosemary's Baby*. LaVey kept a pet lion, a hangover from his days spent as big cat trainer with a circus; he claimed to have prayed down demons on Haight-Ashbury – hippy enclave of San Francisco – and he conducted Satanist baptisms, weddings and funerals. As the High Priest of the movement, he composed both *The Satanic Bible*, published in 1969 and *The Satanic Rituals*, published in 1972. His church was a black house with black windows and black curtains. Inside, he kept a collection of coffins, skeletons, whips and other such weird or fetishistic paraphernalia.

According to LaVey, 'God exists as a universal force, a balancing force in nature and He is far too impersonal to care one whit whether we live or die.' Satan, on the other hand, he saw as 'a symbolic personal saviour, who takes care of mundane fleshly things'. LaVey believed man's true nature was one of lust, hedonism, pride and, above all, wilfulness. It was these attributes, he claimed, that transformed man into a civilized being.

Hollywood film star Jayne Mansfield was one of LaVey's most celebrated followers. The story goes that Mansfield's lawyer, Sam Brody, was upset by her relationship with LaVey for fear it would bring her bad publicity. LaVey, upset by Brody's hostility, put a curse on the lawyer and told Mansfield to stay away from him. Shortly afterwards, Brody was involved in a car accident. LaVey then informed Mansfield that Brody would be involved in another car accident and that she, too, might be injured. Mansfield took no heed of his warning and in June 1967 both she and Brody

were killed when the car they were in collided with a truck.
Mansfield was decapitated.

If this was not a sign of the power of Satan, what was?
The point was that Satanism promised results, and often
looked as if it got them. Christianity, on the other hand,
concentrated on rewards in the hereafter, and in the sixties
– the decade renowned for expectations of instant
gratification – the hereafter was simply too long to wait.

There was another aspect to Satanism which was
particularly appealing to the sixties' generation. According
to LaVey, 'There is a demon inside man. It must be exercised
not exorcized.' Christianity for many seemed to spell
repression. It could scarcely be expected to capture the
imagination of those who believed in 'letting it all hang out'.
The seven deadly sins were, LaVey assured his followers,
'invented by the Christian Church to ensure guilt on the
part of their followers'. And guilt spelt bondage, not
liberation. 'As a Satanist,' promised LaVey, 'you will learn
to indulge in the so-called seven deadly sins, since they all
lead to physical or mental gratification.'

In the same way, the Process Church of the Final
Judgement promised liberation of a therapeutic variety. The
Process Church was founded in London in 1963 by two
former followers of the Church of Scientology, itself a
strange cult blending religion and therapy. *Satan on War*,
a book promoting the Process Church, encouraged followers
to 'Release the fiend that lies dormant within you, for he
is strong and ruthless and his power is far beyond the bounds
of human frailty.' Apparently, when the day of the Final
Judgment arrived, Christ and Satan would together wipe
out the 'Grey Forces' of moderation.

Satanism, then, offered glamour, exoticism, permissiveness, liberation and power. In comparison, Christianity looked decidedly mediocre and half-baked. Christians might talk about being 'set free' from 'occult bondage', but from the viewpoint of the sixties' generation – and you have to remember the decade had been dubbed the 'liberated sixties' – Christianity seemed to offer little more than a straitjacket.

It is hard not to view the histrionics that accompany some – though by no means all – exorcisms as a direct challenge to the seeming razzmatazz of Satanism. Both Christianity and Satanism promised freedom. The battle was on to see who could make their offer seem most compelling and attractive. The rise in Satanism and the flurry of demonic horror films produced both a rise in the number of people seeking exorcisms and a challenge to the Christian Church to demonstrate its superior power.

In the mid-seventies, many of Anton LaVey's followers left the Church of Satan to form their own Satanist group. The Church of Satan reorganized itself and went underground, becoming a secret society. Today, although LaVey has long-since relinquished his starring role, membership of the Church of Satan is said to be once again on the rise. Quite what the head-count stands at, nobody can be certain. At its peak in the late sixties membership was put at anything between 25,000 and a million, although even the lower figure is believed to have been wildly exaggerated.

Not everyone attracted to Satanism joins one of the large organizations. And not everyone advertises their wares so stridently as did Anton LaVey. Certainly, residents of a sleepy stockbroker-belt village north of London were blissfully unaware of the bizarre activities which went on within a stone's throw of their neatly mown lawns and well-clipped hedges during the early 1980s.

For most residents of Chalfont St Peter, an evening's excitement might amount at most to a game of bridge or an idle chat over a drink. But this picture-book world allegedly hid a secret beyond the bounds of most people's imagination. The secret was Satanism.

Jim Perry claims he was present at many of the lavish Satanist ceremonies held there, in the cellar of a wealthy, Bentley-driving businessman's family home. Decked out with black hangings, black candles, pentagrams and the head of a goat, the underground room was, he says, easily transformed into a macabre temple. According to Jim, upwards of forty gowned and hooded Satanists regularly gathered here to worship the Prince of Darkness. Helped by his wife, the High Priestess, the businessman would, says Jim, conduct the chilling Black Mass and preside over gruesome rituals involving animal sacrifice and sexual perversion.

But the story of Jim Perry's involvement in Satanism and eventual deliverance therefrom begins long before this. His tale is astounding to the point that it virtually beggars belief. A cheerful, wise-cracking Londoner in his mid-to-late forties, Jim is well aware that people find his story hard to swallow, and peppers his conversation with emphatic claims that what he relates is indeed true.

As he tells it, it all began when he was just eighteen months old.

'I spent the first two years of my life in India, where I was brought up by an Indian nanny,' he begins. 'When I was eighteen months old she took me into a Hindu temple and dedicated me to Shiva, the Hindu god of destruction. My ayah thought that by doing this she would protect me from evil, but in fact by dedicating me to Shiva, she had opened me up to demonic possession.' According to Jim, from that day onwards, he was demonized, although years were to pass before his infant encounter with non-Christian deities bore fruit.

In his early twenties, and by now back in England, Jim began to take an interest in the writings of Aleister Crowley, the controversial occultist who died in 1947 having earned the nickname of 'the Beast', or the Antichrist.

'I started reading Crowley's books and began to meet up with people with similar interests to mine,' Jim recalls. 'Before long, I was invited to join a witches' coven near my home in Uxbridge. I jumped at the opportunity. It promised to be challenging and exciting, and in some ways it certainly was: the women all wore long flowing robes, whereas the men were made to attend the ceremonies naked. As it turned out, however, the coven was simply the outer ring of something much more dangerous – Satanism.'

Intrigued by the promise of something offering yet more power, Jim longed to join the inner circle and eventually managed to get an interview with the top man himself, the Bentley-driving businessman known to his underlings as 'The Master'.

'Before I was granted an audience with him, I had to pass a type of occult test,' Jim continues. 'I was left alone with a powerful Satanist for a few minutes, during which time he gave me a type of psychic test. Obviously, he deemed me suitable material as he passed me on to The Master.'

That, according to Jim, was like meeting a dead man: 'He betrayed absolutely no emotion and his eyes were completely dead. All the same, he told me what I wanted to hear – that I was accepted into the inner circle.'

But before he was actually allowed to attend a Satanist ceremony, Jim had to undergo a long training. He recalls being ordered to complete a daunting reading list, including works by Aleister Crowley and the nineteenth-century French occultist Eliphas Levi. He also says he had to study the work of other occult groups. It was two years before, in 1973, he was finally allowed to become a true Satanist.

'My initiation ceremony took place in a large house – I don't know where, I was blindfolded and driven there,' he explains. 'Then I was left alone in a room while the fully initiated Satanists conducted the Black Mass.'

The Black Mass is a parody of the Catholic Mass. As with other aspects of Satanism, the aim is to reverse the order of Christianity. With the Black Mass, this means that the Christian ritual is performed, at least in part, backwards and the name of Satan is substituted for that of Christ. The crucifix is inverted, urine is sometimes used instead of holy water and blood instead of wine. According to Jim, Satanists believe that in perverting the Christian ritual, they put Christ's power at their disposal. It is, however, a power which Satanists use for evil ends.

Jim had learnt about the Black Mass during his course of study. He knew that as early as the seventh century, priests were condemned by the Catholic Church for striving to use the power of the Holy Mass to curse people. And he knew that in sixteenth-and seventeenth-century France several priests were executed for conducting Black Masses. By the late seventeenth century, the Black Mass had become fashionable as an erotic pastime for the rich. When the scandal finally broke, more than two hundred arrests were made. In England, the Hellfire Club, a group of rich men with time on their hands, also used the Black Mass as an excuse for an orgy.

The group of Satanists Jim was about to join certainly enjoyed the erotic aspects of the Black Mass: 'A naked woman always lay on the altar and held the cup into which the blood of a sacrificial animal – a cat, dog or goat was drained,' he recalls. 'Then The Master, if he so wished, would have his way with her. Usually the other men could, too.' But Jim insists that Satanism is not simply an excuse for sexual frolics, and claims that on the night of his initiation, far more serious affairs were on the agenda.

'After the Black Mass had been conducted, I was brought into the special chamber. The Master laid hands on me and placed demons inside me. Then I had to read out the Satanist oath: "With this oath sworn under the names of Beelzebub, Baal and Ashtoreth I surrender myself totally to the Lord Satan. I declare myself ready to do his bidding whatever that may be. I give myself body, soul and spirit to Satan." Finally, I had to sign the oath with my blood and I was given a new name. Nobody in the group knew each other's real names: they were too afraid of blackmail.'

Among the demons Jim claims he was given were those of divination, addiction, spite and hate. He insists that they were demons rather than simply habits or feelings, explaining: 'I wasn't simply feeling hateful, I was deliberately given a demon of hate and I deliberately invited that demon of hate to enter me.'

Demon possession, according to Jim, bears no comparison to being possessed by Satan. He has, he says, only once in his life had to suffer that: 'It lasted about an hour or an hour and a half, during one of our ceremonies,' he recalls, 'Satan completely took me over. Most demons will whisper in your ear and say "Do this, do that" but when Satan enters you, you lose everything, your whole mind is blacked out. You don't feel scared, you don't feel anything. During the time that I was fully possessed by Satan, I have no idea what happened, I haven't a clue what I got up to. It frightens me to think what I might have done.'

According to Gordon Melton, an American academic specializing in new religious movements, Satanism can be divided into two main schools. He writes in his *Encyclopedia of Religions*:

As one studies the contemporary Satanist scene, two distinct realities emerge. On the one hand are what are frequently termed the 'sickies'. These are disconnected groups of occultists who employ Satan worship to cover a variety of sexual, sado-masochistic, clandestine, psychopathic, and illegal activities . . . These groups are characterized by lack of theology, disconnectedness and short life, and informality of meetings. Usually they are discovered only in the incident that destroys them. On the other hand are the public groups which take Satanism as a religion seriously . . . While, theologically, the Christian might find both reprehensible, their behaviour is drastically different and the groups should not be confused.

In which camp, then, did Jim's Satanist group fall? He believes the distinction is far from being clear-cut. While some people might initially be drawn to the cocktail of sex and ritual on offer from Satanism, he says these same people soon become equally entranced by the sense of power they derive from worshipping the Devil. On the other hand, he says, those who take Satanism as a serious religion will inevitably be drawn into performing sexual perversions and carrying out illegal activities. As far as Jim is concerned, all forms of Satanism cause those involved to become possessed by demons and the Devil – and all forms of Satanism can only be 'cured' by deliverance.

Following Jim's initiation to the full rank of Satanist, he regularly attended meetings – sometimes two or three times a week, always at least once a month.

'We would help each other with curses or spells,' he recalls, adding emphatically that they most definitely worked. 'I would make voodoo dolls and stick pins in them where I wanted my enemy to suffer. One man outside our circle began to spread stories about me and so I gave him laryngitis by sticking a pin in a doll's throat. After the serious business, most meetings would end with an orgy and a big meal.'

Occasionally, Satanists from other parts of the country would come and visit Jim's group and report to its members on their progress. The talk was often of recruitment campaigns, and from the information he gleaned, Jim now puts the number of Satanists in Britain at about thirty or forty thousand.

Such an estimate wildly exceeds that given by many other experts. But precise figures are hard to come by. One guide to the sorts of numbers involved can be gleaned from *The Occult Census*, a survey carried out in 1989 by The Sorcerer's Apprentice, an occult centre in Leeds. The census revealed that of the one thousand respondents, forty held 'a committed belief in Satanism'.

The Occult Census also claimed that the average occultist is aged thirty-two, college educated, ecologically minded, Green, Liberal or Democrat, a house owner, a *Guardian* or *Independent* reader and bookish. In addition, it said, they tend to be skilled or professional workers, prone 'to believe in the efficacy of spells'.

According to Chris Bray, who orchestrated the census:

> The number of people with a serious and calculated interest in Mystical and magickal things is growing by leaps and bounds . . . Occultists are usually MORE successful and talented at what they do (because of their special training) . . . Occultists believe that the refinement of life energies, talents and abilities through occult technology can rapidly assist the development of our society. (1)

While only the merest smattering of occultists are Satanists, the promise of worldly success is certainly one of Satanism's attractions.

Time and again former Satanists claim that present-day Satanism attracts rich and influential followers. According to Jim, his own Satanist temple included in its number two stockbrokers, a bank manager, and an army colonel.

'Because Satanism is steeped in power and manipulation, it often attracts people in high positions,' he explains. 'They are hooked on the idea of being able to turn events to their own advantage, however it might hurt other people. The reason why we don't hear more about the more horrific side of Satanism is that so many Satanists hold the reins of power.'

One self-styled exorcist claims that he occasionally receives anxious telephone calls from individuals claiming a 'top Satanist' has put a curse on them.

'I ask them where the supposed Satanist lives and what kind of car he drives,' he says. 'Unless they reply that he lives in a mansion and drives a Rolls – or something to the equivalent – I tell them not to worry. Satanists are in the business of acquiring wealth and status. Any Satanist who fails in this respect isn't worthy of the name.'

An alternative thesis is that the wealth and prestige story is put around by Satanists who wish to win more followers to their ranks – and by ex-Satanists who wish to glamorize their former lifestyle.

Jim is, however, adamant in his claims. He insists that the five most powerful Satanists in Britain – capable, he says, of murdering using their magic alone – include a top civil servant, a well-known author and a bank manager. A story repeatedly told in the late 1980s was that a British politician was being investigated by the police for his Satanist activities – a move which many regarded as an unprecedented coup since the authorities generally refuse to treat such accusations seriously. No revelations have so far come to light, however.

The lure of Satanism was certainly sufficient to attract Jim. Three years later, however, something happened to bring about a dramatic change.

In July 1984, Jim was living in a shared house in north London. Among the other tenants was Veronica, a committed Christian. That month, Luis Palau, the Christian evangelist, was holding a mission at Queen's Park Rangers football ground and Veronica persuaded Jim to join her there one evening. 'I thought "Why not?",' says Jim. 'I thought that, as a Satanist, I might at any rate be able to cause some mischief and so I went along with her.' According to Jim, that evening he actually saw spiritual warfare in action.

'To begin with, the Devil appeared to me above the stadium as a beautiful, good-looking character with flowing hair,' he recalls. 'He had a malevolent expression on his face, though, and when the Christians stood up and started singing, you could see how angry he became. Then Satan disappeared and I saw another being. I think it was an archangel, and the peace that came with that vision was fantastic.'

A few nights later, Jim came in from work at about midnight. That day, he says, he had been particularly troubled by the voices of demons and he had finally decided to attempt to get rid of them for ever.

'I stood in my room trying to say, "Satan leave me," and all I could say was "Satan . . . Satan . . . Satan",' he recalls. 'At length I called on Jesus to help me. I felt a weight lifting off my shoulders. It was, I imagine, something like having a whalebone corset removed. Afterwards, I felt a surge of tremendous power and the demons went, just like that. I think they were caught on the hop – and you have to remember there were other Christians in the house who by now were regularly praying for me. That night, I didn't go to sleep. I stayed up and read the Bible – all the wonderful, joyful psalms.'

On Friday, July 13th, Jim decided to go back and see Luis Palau again. On passing through the turnstile at Queen's Park Rangers football ground, he picked up a programme and saw that the subject of the evening's talk was 'Jesus Christ versus the Occult'. It seemed like too much of a coincidence. At the end of the meeting Luis Palau called forward all those who wanted to make a commitment to Christ.

'I was the first one on the pitch,' says Jim. 'After I had

made my commitment, I spoke with a counsellor. When I told him I had been involved in Satanism he delivered me – he prayed over me for about ten minutes. He prayed that all the demons would be gone, and stay gone, and that all the doorways which had previously given entrance to the demons would be broken. I went away walking on air. I felt totally free, completely free. It was just a simple prayer, but it is always the simple prayers that work.'

It was not, however, the end of the demons. Jim and Veronica were married in 1986, but before that Veronica believes she herself was invaded by the same demons that had attacked her husband-to-be.

'I was already a Christian but after meeting Jim I began to be oppressed by demons,' she says. 'Satan was attacking me, and after Jim had been delivered, the demonic assaults on me became even stronger. I am convinced Satan was angry with me for having led Jim to Christ.'

According to Veronica, Satan also did his best to ruin their honeymoon in Crete. 'We were in bed together, having sex, when I heard a voice saying "I am going to destroy your marriage," ' she recalls. 'I was frightened, and afterwards I found it more and more difficult being a Christian. Satan really had it in for me for what I had done.'

Jim readily admits that by now he had become an overwhelmingly zealous Christian, seeking to tell people of his miraculous deliverance from Satan at every turn. Before long, he and Veronica began to attend the London Healing Mission in London's Notting Hill, a Christian centre led by the Reverend Andy Arbuthnot whom we shall meet more thoroughly in a later chapter. There, Jim discovered that he had a special gift – the discernment of spirits.

At one of the Healing Mission's Thursday services,

Veronica and Jim were sitting in the congregation holding hands as they watched the Rev Arbuthnot attempting to deal with a man who was, so the gathered assembly believed, possessed.

'You could see the sweat on Andy's brow as he attempted to wrestle with the demon in the man,' Jim recalls. 'Then suddenly I saw, I was given the gift of discernment. I saw a demon sitting on the man's head. It had a spider's body and three heads. Then a voice told me that the demon was Asmodeus, one of the Dukes of Hell, a demon of destruction whose purpose is to destroy mankind.'

Asmodeus is traditionally held to be one of the chief demons involved in cases of possession. He originates from Persian mythology but was absorbed into Hebrew mythology where he is sometimes said to be the offspring of Lilith and Adam. Mentioned in the Apocrypha, Asmodeus leads a legion of lesser demons. One of his chief aims is to prevent intercourse between husband and wife – which perhaps accounts for Veronica's honeymoon experience. Certainly, if he is to be believed, Jim was up against a fearsome enemy.

'All of a sudden,' he continues, 'I was being used as a channel through which to destroy this terrifying being. I was stunned. At the time I didn't know what was happening but I know now that the Holy Spirit was using me as a channel through which he could zap the demon. Andy suddenly switched from wrestling with the demon to praising the Lord – the battle was over. Afterwards, when the spirit had been cast out, Veronica's hand was all bruised because I had been gripping it so tightly.'

According to Jim, the gift of discernment comes and goes, 'It is given and taken away, given and taken away,' he says.

'Otherwise, you would be seeing demons all over the place all day long.'

It was one of the Reverend Arbuthnot's deputies who, says Jim, eventually completed his deliverance. 'He came over to our house with his wife. While he counselled me, his wife counselled Veronica, who was still having trouble with demons. It was at this point that we were both fully delivered. We simply repeated the baptism promises.' Again, the feeling was one of freedom, as if a huge weight was being lifted from them, they say.

But why had Jim not been fully released from the bonds of Satan by his first deliverance? According to the Reverend Trevor Dearing, virtually all exorcisms should be brief and instantly effective. For Jim, the question is easily answered: he had become a Christian back at the Luis Palau mission, but he had not become a sufficiently committed Christian. Jim now believes that if any Christian fails to mount a constant campaign against Satan, they are laying themselves open for demonic possession.

Deliverance can be instantaneous or it can take many months,' he explains. 'It depends on how fully the person has accepted Jesus as Lord, how well they have protected themselves from Satan's onslaughts.'

Apparently, places as well as people need protection. Although Jim and Veronica are highly sceptical of the efficacy of ritual and regalia in destroying demons, they regularly protect their house from demonic infestation by saying prayers in every room. In doing so, they believe they are preventing Satan and his demons from squeezing their way in. It is not a practice which they believe they alone require: in their view, every home needs a regular spiritual clean.

Another alleged means of entrance for demons is through the family line: it is a common belief in some Christian circles that demons can be inherited. The basis for this belief lies in a passage from Deuteronomy, Chapter 5, Verse 9: '. . . for I the Lord thy God am a jealous God, visiting the iniquity of the fathers upon the children unto the third and fourth generation of them that hate me.'

Again, in Exodus Chapter 4, Verse 7, the Lord speaks to Moses of 'visiting the iniquity of the fathers upon the children, and upon the children's children, unto the third and to the fourth generation.'

This, according to some Christians, is unequivocal proof that demons can be passed down through the family, rather like a particular physical characteristic. Jim Perry believes that demons are actually physically transmitted from one generation to the next, often at the time of the new generation's conception, through sexual intercourse. Others say they are passed on at the time of a person's death. The Reverend Selwyn Hughes of the evangelical Crusade for World Renewal, based in Surrey, is less graphic, but none the less does not mince matters. In *The Christian Counsellor* magazine he writes:

It is worth mentioning . . . that if one's family (parents, grandparents, great-grandparents) have dabbled deeply in the occult, this can sometimes open the door to the activity of evil spirits and, even though they may not actually reside in the personalities of children, they can 'hang on', as it were, in the family line. My own view is that where this is so, the influence of demons is dissipated by the third and fourth generation. (2)

With such an apparent plethora of openings to possession at large, exorcists clearly have their work cut out. But the question of a person's suitability for that work has to be raised. How is someone deemed suitable for such a ministry, fraught as it is with countless potential pitfalls? For Jim and Veronica, the answer is simply: they were called by God to become exorcists. And, as with the gift of discernment, who can argue with divine direction?

Jim and Veronica started their own deliverance ministry in 1992. It was, they insist, not something they sought out, but rather something which was thrust upon them as more and more people came to them asking for help.

'We kept asking God whether this was what he intended for us; we kept saying "Surely you can't mean it?" But people kept phoning us and saying they had heard we had started a deliverance ministry. In the end, we decided that this must be what God wanted us to do.'

It must, however, be said that Jim and Veronica had by now become accustomed to touring churches and Christian fellowship meetings telling the gathered assemblies the story of their past. It is not hard to see how their experiences might strike terror into the hearts of all those who listened, increasingly aghast, to the countless ways in which, according to Jim and Veronica, Satan or one of his demons might wriggle a way into them.

Soon the couple began to ask members of their audience who believed they might be demonized to come and see them at the end of the meeting. 'We found there were indeed people at our meetings who were demonized,' says Jim. 'We have even had demons thrown at us from people in the audience.' And so the seeds of their deliverance ministry were sown. Now, they claim to receive up to three enquiries about their ministry each day.

'One case we are currently dealing with is that of a man who has been into Satanism and witchcraft in Wales,' Jim says. 'The group he was with subsidized his drug-taking and so he found it very difficult to get away from them. Eventually, the group decided he was getting too expensive for them and so they set him up as the next human sacrifice. Another member of the group warned him what was going to happen and so he escaped. A Christian came across him and brought him to us. We had to deliver him of five demons of witchcraft. The demons were holding hands and forming a band around his body. We broke their hold and kicked them out and then we got the man to say "Jesus Christ who is the son of God, who died on the cross at Calvary is Lord." If he had still been demonized, he wouldn't have been able to say that. Finally we sealed him by making the mark of the cross on his forehead in oil. He was overjoyed, he was dancing and praising the Lord, but there is still work to be done with him. He isn't fully delivered yet.'

It can be seen that Jim and Veronica are at variance with the Reverend Trevor Dearing who believes that exorcisms should be short and to the point. Perhaps God gives different directions to different people. Or perhaps, as in virtually any field, it is simply that the experts are divided.

Jim and Veronica will not deliver just anyone. Once again, Jim's 'gift of discernment' is called to the fore.

'We have to discern whether we should free the person of a demon or not,' he says. 'If the person is not a Christian, then we might refuse to deliver them because they will end up being far worse off. In the Bible it says that after a demon has been cast out, if the house isn't made secure, seven more demons will enter: I would far rather meet someone with one demon in them than someone with seven demons in them.'

Following the act of deliverance, Veronica and Jim aim to pass the 'freed' person back to their local church provided, they say, that church has the 'right sort of minister' one who is of a fundamentalist and charismatic persuasion. According to Jim, 'We simply do not have time to provide follow-up care to everybody who is delivered by us. Satanism is on the rise and we are becoming busier by the day.'

Jim and Veronica have no training in the deliverance ministry. They believe their personal experiences and the power of God are sufficient to see them through. They have, however, attended a three-day Christian counselling course run by the evangelical Crusade for World Renewal and they are both counsellors for Billy Graham. Although they currently attend an Anglican church, they say they are happy to go along to any place of worship which preaches from the Bible and is spirit-based.

The Reverend Simon Gibson trains counsellors at the Crusade for World Renewal. He has also developed a ministry of deliverance. But whereas Jim Perry and Veronica seem to have been drawn to the ministry through Jim's encounters with the powers of darkness, it was his encounter with the power of God that provided Simon's calling.

Dapper and slightly built with a rakish moustache and cheerful handkerchief neatly folded in the breast pocket of his blazer, Simon appears more suited to the role of a mildly eccentric P.G. Wodehouse character than to that of minister. But the path of Christian service was mapped out to him from an early age.

As a young boy, Simon was an avowed atheist, believing anyone with religious beliefs to be 'sad and pathetic'. One day, as he was sitting around pondering his future and wondering what to do with his life, he was struck by a vision of Christ.

'It was not simply some internal sensation,' he recalls. 'It was very very real. He was standing quite near to me, surrounded by a tremendous light and sense of love and wearing a white robe which reached down to his feet. I couldn't make out the features of his face because it was hidden by a shining light, but I knew that He was calling me to serve Him.'

The supernatural visitation had a profound affect on Simon: 'My life turned round. I had seen God and had responded to Him in my heart.' He was instantly converted to Christianity and eagerly set about seeking out a form of worship which attracted him. His first experience of God having been supernatural, Simon was naturally drawn towards the charismatic movement and was baptized in the spirit in the late seventies.

During the mid-1980s, Simon's life once again received divine direction.

'One day, my wife and I were praying and the Lord gave each of us the word "Pentecostal",' he recalls. 'We didn't know what it meant at first but we eventually found ourselves members of a Pentecostal Church.'

In 1987, Simon received ordination within the Elim Pentecostal Church. The Pentecostal movement originated in the United States in the early twentieth century. Its emphasis is on spiritual renewal through baptism in the Holy Spirit and so Simon was an ideal candidate for its ranks.

'Some denominations have tended to overlook the Holy

Spirit,' says Simon. 'Pentecostal Churches have helped to engender a more balanced theology. For them, deliverance ministry is an important part of their work.'

Whereas many Christians struggle constantly for faith, Simon had, he believes, been given concrete evidence of God. And just as he had been convinced of the reality of a supernatural God, so he quickly came to believe in the reality of a supernatural Devil and demons.

There is an ongoing debate among some Christians as to how long these supposed demons have been around. Most agree, however, that they have been plaguing mankind since the fall of Satan from heaven. Some say this occurred before the creation of man, others that it happened in the early days of man's appearance on earth. Simon remains undecided on the matter. But he believes that, 'Down through the centuries these demons have been present on earth and their influence can vary from generation to generation according to how open human beings are to their influence.' At the moment, he adds, Western society is experiencing a rise in this influence.

Some Christians seem to welcome the alleged spiralling onslaught of Satan and his troops. For them, it is a sign that we are in the Last Days, and that the tremendous battle of Armageddon which signals Christ's Second Coming is imminent. As they prepare themselves for the fight, they are secure in the knowledge that they will receive a string of medals for their undaunted courage.

According to Hal Lindsey, author of blockbuster best sellers on the spiritual battle to come: 'Not many believers are called upon to endure direct Satanic attack in the way that Job was. Only those who are specially prepared and called are thrust into that conflict. But rest assured that these battle-tested warriors will be given special veteran rewards.' (3)

Simon dates the renewed vigour of Satan's onslaught to the repeal of the Witchcraft Act in the 1950s.

'Since then, there has been a dramatic increase in Satanism and the occult,' he says. 'As a result, the demonic forces which surround us have gained a wider influence. Christianity's place in our society has been undermined and we have seen a breakdown in morality.'

Witches hotly dispute that they have any truck with Satanism, but it is an accusation which Christians down the centuries have repeatedly made – and continue to make today.

Simon is convinced that demons currently hold an increasing sway over human beings. He does not believe, however, that this means they have increased in number. Again, this is a point over which Christians argue. According to Revelations, Chapter 10, Verses 13-14, an angel is ordered to 'Loose the four angels which are bound in the great river Euphrates.' The angel does as told 'And the four angels were loosed, which were prepared for an hour, and a day, and a month, and a year, for to slay the third part of men.' Some Christians believe that this event has already occurred, that the angels – in this instance fallen angels, or demons – have been released from captivity in the River Euphrates and have added their strength to the demonic onslaught against mankind.

The precise nature of demons is another moot point for Christians. Simon believes that demons bear a number of similarities to human beings.

'They appear to have intelligence, to be capable of thought and to have particular identities,' he says. These identities are, he adds, 'basically malevolent' . . . 'What demons lack', he continues, 'are physical bodies, although very often they seek embodiment in human beings.' Again, some Christians believe that demons can only operate through human beings – that they must enter a human being before they can have any influence over them. According to Simon, however, demons can communicate with people at a mental level. He refers to Satan's temptation of Jesus in the wilderness where it seems that Satan communicated with Jesus without requiring the mediation of another human being.

According to Dr Merrill Unger, author of *Demons in the World Today*: 'Demons believe, but only tremble. They are confirmed in depravity and never seek forgiveness. They are unclean and never long for purity. They confess Jesus Christ as Lord, but they do not trust Christ or submit to him, although they obviously recognize his authority.' (4)

Debate also rages over whether or not it is possible for places to have demons. In the Book of Daniel, Daniel has prayed and is waiting for an answer from God. After about two weeks the angel comes to him and says he was resisted by the Prince of Persia. According to some Christians, this means that Persia was ruled over by its own specific demon. Then, in Revelations, God tells John to write to the seven churches. In the letter to the church in Pergamos, Chapter Two, Verse 13, he is told to write: 'I know thy works, and where thou dwellest, even where Satan's seat is . . .' Some Christians interpret this literally, as stating that Satan's headquarters on earth were at Pergamos, an ancient Greek city in what is now Turkey. Others interpret the passage as meaning simply that the inhabitants of Pergamos were straying from God's path.

Many Christians viewed the Gulf War as a Holy War and, through prayer, attempted to combat the Spirit of Babylon which they believed to be geographically located in Iraq. In summer 1990, for example, an international Christian prayer team visited Iraq, prayed for the protection of Israel and asked God to execute judgment over Iraq. The members of the team had all, apparently, been called by the Lord through the following passage from Micah, Chapter 5:

> . . . when the Assyrian shall come into our land: and when he shall tread in our palaces, then shall we raise against him seven shepherds, and eight principal men. And they shall waste the land of Assyria with the sword, and the land of Nimrod in the entrances thereof: thus shall he deliver us from the Assyrian, when he cometh into our land, and when he treadeth within our borders.

As it turned out, the prayer team consisted of seven pastors and eight laymen. They journeyed throughout Iraq, and claimed to enter all the cities of Nimrod with a spiritual sword of prayer. Lo and behold, 'Within forty days of this spiritual action Iraq invaded Kuwait and current events in that area began.' (5) Equally miraculously, Iraq was eventually defeated.

Prayer warfare is judged to be perhaps the key weapon in the Christian's armoury. According to Jessie Penn-Lewis:

> Briefly, prayer warfare simply means holding unceasingly the power of the 'finished work of Christ' over the hosts of evil, in their attack upon some place or person, until the victory is won. Just as Moses lifted his hands steadfastly

until the victory was won so the prayer warrior holds up steadfastly the victory of the Cross – the finished victory of Christ over Satan – until the forces of evil retreat and are vanquished.' (6)

Simon veers towards the belief that particular places can have demons: 'Only God is omnipresent and so Satan and his demons would appear to be localized,' he explains. The difficulty then arises that Satan can only be active in one place at one time. When, for instance, Martin Luther speaks of having encountered Satan one evening – and having dismissed him by throwing his ink pot at him – then Satan could not have been anywhere else at that particular time. Perhaps the explanation lies in Simon's belief that people can become habituated to evil: 'Someone may be influenced by Satan or a demon,' he says. 'In time, that direct Satanic or demonic influence will become learnt and so the demon can pack his bag and go.'

Simon's unwavering belief in the reality of supernatural powers is matched by his conviction that we are all spiritual beings and as a result are all, at one time or another, going to hear from demons.

'Because we are spiritual beings, we will all hear from the spiritual realm, whether or not we recognize it as such,' he says, adding: 'Sometimes God will be talking to us, sometimes Satan or demons will be talking to us.'

According to John White, author of *The Fight*, the bloody battles and appalling atrocities of mere earthly warfare fade into insignificance when compared with the continual thunderous clash of spiritual warfare: 'War is not something that illustrates aspects of Christian living. Christian living is war. Indeed I would go further,' he says, and does: 'Earthly warfare is not the real warfare. It is but a faint, ugly reflection of the real thing.' (7)

Simon believes that he himself is constantly engaged in spiritual warfare:

'I have felt the intensity of the battle and I have had to face demonic forces,' he declares. During such times of crisis, he will pray to God and ask to be shown what is happening: 'I will get a revelation from God which will diffuse the spiritual conflict and release me from the warfare.' He frequently finds that such times of conflict will occur during the lead-up to a difficult deliverance.

Before stumbling across his first case of someone in need of deliverance, Simon had not been taught how the ministry should be conducted. But, with the Bible as his guide, he believed that, 'If there are demonic forces present and they are troubling people, then they can be commanded to leave in Jesus's name – they must obey the name of Jesus.' Looking back, he feels that though he still believes this to be true, his initial approach was a little simplistic.

'Subsequent experience has shown me that releasing people from the influence of demonic forces is not always as straightforward as that. I believe that the spiritual realm, the psychological realm and the physical realm are all intimately related and that all three should be taken into account before conducting a deliverance.'

For this reason, although Simon believes that it is in the power of any Christian to rebuke and cast out demons in Jesus's name, he feels there are those who are particularly called to the ministry. He himself claims to have a particular knack for discerning the root of a person's problem.

'A woman suffering from severe stress and anxiety and who thought she might be under demonic influence once asked me to pray for her,' he recalls. 'As we prayed, a picture emerged to me of a face on a balloon. When I told the woman what I had seen, she was amazed: some time ago she had been involved with a cult group whose members were told to empty their minds and then meditate on this being in the form of a balloon. We prayed together that if this cult involvement had allowed a demonic influence into her life, it would be broken. From that point on she had no more trouble.'

On another occasion, Simon was confronted by a young man who suffered from extreme shyness and was unable to relate to people.

'I was counselling him and looking at the problem from all kinds of angles but we just weren't breaking through,' he says. 'Eventually I suggested to him that we pray together and see what God said to us. As we prayed, I had a picture of pyramids and Egyptian symbols. I wondered whether this was God or my imagination at work but I told the young man what I had seen. He said that when he was a child he had watched a film about Egypt. The following day, he was driving in the car with his parents when he saw the sun and he found himself overwhelmingly drawn to it – he simply could not take his eyes away.'

Remembering that sun worship played an important part in Egyptian religion, Simon guessed that the man was under the demonic influence of pagan beliefs.

'We prayed again and I said that if demonic entities were influencing the young man through the Egyptian religion, we took authority over them in the name of Jesus and broke their power. Afterwards, there was a dramatic change in the young man's life. His inhibitions were gone and for the first time in years he could relate to other people.'

Simon views the pictures he receives as a kind of God-sent vision intended to aid him in his ministry. On other occasions, he receives more direct messages from God. He recalls how a man troubled by terrible fears came to him for help and during the counselling session began to speak in a strange voice.

'The voice was a lot slower and deeper than the man's and talked about having come to Britain from across the sea. I recognized that it was the voice of a demon and it threw me completely. I prayed to God, asking for help and the Lord told me to fast for three or four days. At the end of this time, the Lord told me that this was the time to minister and so I met the man and prayed over him and commanded this being to leave. It did as I commanded.'

Like the Reverend Trevor Dearing, however, Simon believes that apparent manifestations of demonization can sometimes be misleading. Following a dinner for Christian businessmen which Simon attended, one of the diners began to scream and wail but would not come forward to receive prayer.

'The other people at the dinner thought he was possessed but I wasn't at all sure what was going on,' Simon confesses. 'I prayed for him but there was no change at all in his behaviour: he carried on crying and screaming. Suddenly it clicked: I got the distinct impression that this was a form of attention-seeking behaviour and so I advised everyone to leave him alone. He soon stopped carrying on.'

Among the indications of demonization or possible possession that Simon looks out for are excessive fear, the tendency to speak in a strange voice that seems to reflect an identity other than that of the person, and foaming at the mouth. Simon also believes that often, when a person is demonized, there will be something strange about their eyes. He cites the case of someone whom he believes to be under the influence of evil spirits.

'When I am talking to him, his eyes roll back and for a time, all you can see is the whites of his eyes. I don't believe this person is possessed, but I do believe he needs to be set free from some malign spiritual influence.'

Before embarking on a deliverance Simon will devote considerable time to counselling the individual.

'The number one rule for me is to be absolutely certain that the problem is demonic and that deliverance would be the most loving ministry I could possibly offer the person. To begin with I will collect certain data about the person such as their background, their current situation and a variety of psychological factors. At the end of the day, however, I would need to feel a conviction from God that they were suffering from a problem caused by a demonic entity.'

If this conviction is not forthcoming, Simon will say a blanket prayer for the person. 'At the end of a counselling session I may well pray that if there are spiritual forces binding the person I am dealing with, that those forces will be bound and sent away.'

During the deliverance itself, Simon never follows a set liturgical form. Instead, he attempts to be sensitive to God and to act as God's mouthpiece.

'I put myself at God's disposal,' he says. 'My heart's desire is to be a channel for God's redeeming work.'

Looking back over what he does actually say, however, he recognizes that he repeatedly uses certain words and phrases: he takes authority over the demonic forces, he binds them and in Jesus's name he breaks their power over the person's life. Finally, he often prays that the demons will be consigned to whatever place God has in mind for them.

The precise location of this place is another question which plagues some Christians. According to some readings of the Bible, demons surround us all the time, thronging the air and hovering expectantly in the hope of tripping us up. In Ephesians, Chapter 2, Verse 2 Paul refers to 'the prince of the power of the air', in Chapter 3, Verse 10 to 'principalities and powers in heavenly places', and in Chapter 6, Verse 12 to the 'rulers of the darkness of the world'.

But according to the Bible, not all demons are waiting gleefully to ambush us. Some are already confined in gruesome prisons awaiting the final judgment. In the book of Jude, Verse 6, we are told that 'the angels which kept not their first estate, but left their own habitation, he hath reserved in everlasting chains under darkness unto the judgment of the great day.' And in 2 Peter, Chapter 2 Verse 4, we are told that 'God spared not the angels that sinned, but cast them down to hell, and delivered them into chains of darkness, to be reserved unto judgment.'

Perhaps it is to this hellhole that Luke refers in his account of the story of the Gadarene demoniac. According to his version of the tale, the demons begged Jesus not to send them 'out into the deep' (8). In Mark's account of the same story, however, the demons, before entering the swine, ask not to be sent away 'out of the country'. (9)

Simon is uncertain of the precise destination of exorcized demons. If, he says, they are sent to hell, then this would suggest that exorcists are slowly but surely ridding the world of demons. He has grave doubts as to whether this can really be the case. The fact that Jesus sent the demons possessing the Gadarene demoniac into a herd of swine rather than to hell perhaps suggests that Jesus was undertaking a first offensive against the demons, whereas their final defeat has yet to come.

Until that time should arise, many Christians believe more and more people are being tempted to join Satan's swelling army. They claim that the recruitment campaign is being effected not through the lure of Satanism itself, but in a much more subtle way: through enticing people down the path of darkness with seemingly harmless games.

3

It All Began With A Ouija Board

It was during his student days in the mid 1970s that Simon Gibson performed his first act of deliverance. His neighbours had become interested in tarot cards and began to read people's fortunes. Sometimes, they would invite people round to their house in the evening and hold fortune-telling parties. Although they knew Simon was a committed Christian, they were quite open with him about their new pastime – they saw nothing wrong with it. Simon was not so sure and warned them that it might lead to trouble. They took no notice of him.

'One day, the couple came to my house in terrible consternation,' Simon recalls. 'They said awful things were happening in their home – that furniture was moving around and that their casement windows were moving up and down. Almost without thinking, I told them not to worry and said I would come round and pray over the house. When I got there, I didn't see any activity myself but the couple were clearly immensely distressed. I walked in and very simply I commanded any evil presence to leave. I told the couple that their so-called hobby had opened up their home to invasion by evil spirits and advised them to put a stop to it unless they wanted a repeat performance. They did as I advised, and from then on, the trouble ceased.'

In *The Exorcist*, it is not explicitly stated how the young girl Regan becomes possessed. She has, however, taken to playing with a Ouija board.

In recent years, it has become a stock-in-trade of many Christians to cite the Ouija board as a standard means by which people can open themselves up to possession by evil spirits. The game, played by countless schoolchildren throughout the country as a means of whiling away their lunch breaks, is supposed to relay messages from the beyond. Most children enjoy the slightly scary thrill the game gives them; according to many Christians, it can give them a good deal more than they bargained for.

The Reverend Russ Parker, an Anglican vicar from Leicestershire, claims to have counselled a number of people, including children, who 'have been deeply disturbed at what happened when "playing" this deadly game.' He insists that the power behind the board does indeed communicate with the living.

> In one case, a local minister was called in to a school where some pupils were in a hysterical and suicidal state, frightened by their experience of this game ... Ouija, along with books on magic and the supernatural often lead the curious enquirer into an addiction to things magical and mysterious. They have led people into contact with forces outside of themselves, from which it is very difficult to get free. (1)

According to Roger Ellis who leads the Revelation Christian Fellowship in Sussex, 'Many people have been plagued with fear, depression, rage, anger, insanity and have even attempted to commit suicide after involvement with Ouija. It is to be avoided at all costs.' (2) The Evangelical Alliance of Great Britain, which represents more than a million UK churchgoers, opens its booklet *Doorways to Danger* with the warning: 'A neighbourhood seance. An astrologer's telephone helpline. Teenagers' fun with Ouija boards. These seemingly innocent entertainments could be entrances into a sinister world of evil and destruction.' Ouija, according to the booklet, 'has been likened to inviting a child to build sand castles on a beach laid with land mines. Tragically, there is a Ouija craze in Britain today.' (3)

Set Free!, a booklet published by Christian Response to the Occult, an evangelical group based in London, goes even further in its claims: 'Have you consulted the Ouija board (even out of curiosity), or played with the popular occult games being sold today . . .?' it asks, continuing: 'Are you aware that anyone who has ever practised or participated in any form of occultism (whether done innocently or not) has opened the door to oppression by the powers of darkness, even though such occult activity may have occurred many years ago or before having become a Christian?' Few people can, hand on heart, claim to have desisted from any such activity. The spectre of the powers of darkness looms like the bogeyman of old.

None the less, it seems that many of those who come to believe themselves demonically possessed have at one time or another played with a Ouija board. A typical testimony is that of Sally, a pretty and quick-witted young woman, now a committed Christian.

'My aunt had always been involved in occult activities, including using the Ouija board, and so I was very aware of spiritual matters from early childhood,' she explains. 'I remember doing a project on the supernatural at my public school and I spent hours in the library finding out about things such as ghosts and extrasensory perception. It all fascinated me.'

When she was eighteen, Sally moved to London and began training to become a nurse. She and a group of friends would gather in her room, share a couple of bottles of wine, and play with the Ouija board.

'From the moment I became involved in Ouija it became obvious I was open to spiritual things. It always worked and it became like an addiction. I took the lead in things, and I brought several people into the occult. Of course I knew that some people thought Ouija was dangerous, but as far as I was concerned, that was simply an old granny approach. All I felt was excitement and anticipation, although we did put Bibles at all four corners of the room . . . just in case.'

Sally would ask the Ouija board standard questions such as whether or not she would get married and whether or not she would be happy in life.

'I thought that maybe if I had a framework for my future, something to look forward to, I would be able to get over the depression of broken relationships and long working hours,' she explains. 'I needed security, but I come from a privileged background and I didn't find it in material things.'

As time passed by, Sally became increasingly adept with the Ouija board and claims she soon found she was able to channel spirits without its assistance.

'I had two main spirit guides who took on the characteristics of real people who had lived in the past,' she recalls. 'Some people say the occult is mind over matter, but if you have had any experiences you know that's rubbish: my spirit guides would tell me things that had happened in the past and when I checked the facts, they proved to be true. It was tremendously exciting. I suddenly had all this power – or so I thought. The big lure of the occult of any description is that you think you are in control, but in fact you slowly but surely begin to abdicate your responsibility.'

Sally vividly remembers the first time she became aware that a spirit had entered her.

'I gave physical control of my life to a spirit who claimed to be my dead sister. My mother had miscarried three months before she conceived me and the spirit masqueraded as my sister and said she wanted to live her life through mine. At the time, it seemed an entirely fair proposition and so I decided to give her a go.'

Despite by now believing herself to be thoroughly acquainted with the workings of the occult, Sally was far from prepared for the devilish results of her decision.

'I remember looking in the mirror and noticing that my eyes had changed colour and my face had altered beyond recognition. I began to breathe very heavily and became cold in the middle and hot everywhere else. At that point, I began to laugh and I felt the spirit enter me. I still wasn't frightened, though I entirely believed that the spirit was who it claimed to be. I was convinced that the spirit of my sister would want the best for me.'

To begin with, the spirits would appear only when Sally specifically invoked them. Before long, however, they would take her over at random:

'It got to the point when I would be walking to the shops and suddenly the spirits would start talking to me. They began to take over my life in all sorts of peculiar ways. One of my spirits really liked the colour purple and would tell me what clothes to buy and wear. There were moments when I began to get scared.'

Looking back, Sally now realizes that this marked the

beginning of a period of total confusion. Some of the worst times, she says, were when the spirits began fighting between themselves, each demanding the greatest control over her.

'One spirit would say, "I have control, I am more powerful," and another would say, "You will never be happy until you give yourself totally to me." In a sense it was extremely seductive to have the spirits fighting over me like this. It made me feel important, wanted. Then things began to come to a head and finally I realized I was no longer in control. One time I went into a trance and came round to find I was pointing a knife at myself.'

For some time, the spirits had been telling Sally that she must on no account go to Chichester, the pleasant cathedral city in the south of England where one of her cousins lived. Although puzzled by the instruction, Sally paid it little heed. Then, one day, almost unthinkingly, she defied the spirits. As it turned out, they proved to have had good reason to be worried. Sally's cousin was a member of the Revelation Christian Fellowship, led by the same Roger Ellis already encountered. That Sunday, Sally attended a fellowship meeting. By the trick of fate or grace of God seemingly so often encountered in these situations, Roger chose as the subject of his talk none other than the occult and spiritual warfare.

'I heard God speaking to me,' Sally recalls. 'In just that one meeting I was remarkably free. I asked God into my life and the fellowship members prayed for me and told the demons to depart. From then on my lifestyle changed dramatically.'

The Ouija board is, however, by no means the only superficially harmless pastime which is said to lead the innocent down the slippery slope to possession. Roger Ellis provides an A–Z directory of ways in which people can be ensnared in the occult. It includes numerology, parapsychology, palmistry, levitation, dowsing, drugs and horoscopes. Young, fresh-faced and fashionably dressed, Roger is light years from the stereotype picture of an exorcist many people carry around. But, as with so many of the exorcists we have encountered, it is a ministry which he felt compelled to enter into simply in response to demand.

Roger has, he says, had many people coming to him who have experienced suicidal urges as a result of their occult activity. Some, he says, have been involved in fantasy role playing games such as Dungeons and Dragons and have found themselves taking on the demonic personality of their character in the game. In Dungeons and Dragons the players create their own characters and story-lines following guidelines given to them by the 'Dungeon master'. Repeatedly referred to by Christians as a gateway to the occult, the game has been described as an 'instructional tool' which 'teaches demonology, witchcraft, voodoo, murder, rape, blasphemy, suicide, assassination, insanity, sex perversion, homosexuality, Satan worship, gambling, sadism, desecration, necromancy and divination.'

Other tormented individuals have sought out Roger after visiting mediums or playing with the Ouija board or tarot cards. His conclusion is that 'any contact with the occult is very very dangerous and can lead to possession'. While he points out that not everyone dabbling in the occult is going to become possessed, he insists that the occult has 'a powerful, compulsive effect on people', that there is always 'an addictive element in the occult' and that in coming into contact with the occult, people are 'tapping into dark spiritual forces'. He warns that, while some people might see the occult as a game, that attitude is 'like taking a powerful pill and not believing it will work, whereas of course, whether you believe in the pill or not, it is going to have an affect on you. Where the occult is concerned, some people have had quite a few nasty surprises.'

Roger prefers not to refer to people as being possessed by demons. Instead, he describes them as being 'infiltrated or influenced by evil forces'. He recalls the first time he came across such a case:

'I was in a fellowship meeting and this person suddenly went rigid, hit the floor and started convulsing. There was a doctor there and I looked at him and said, "Is this a fit, or is it something else?" The doctor looked at me and said, "This hasn't got the signs of a fit. Is it evil?" So I prayed. The man was delivered, and later we discovered that he had links with the occult. The evil forces in him must have been provoked by our worship.'

Following that first exorcism, Roger found that more and more people began coming to him for help. He soon realized that, if he were to develop a mature ministry, he would have to do some reading and thinking.

'I read the New Testament carefully, and examined the cases of deliverance there. Then I spoke to one or two people involved in the deliverance ministry and slowly I have moved forward.'

Roger will also pray through people's homes in order to exorcise the evil spirits therefrom: 'Sometimes, the homes of people who are involved in the occult have a very dark sense about them which needs clearing by prayer,' he says.

Unlike Jim and Veronica Perry, Roger will deliver non-Christians.

'If someone is not from a Christian family, I will spend

some time sharing with them my view of occult involvement and possession,' he explains. 'If they are still not interested in becoming a Christian, I tell them that if they want to come out of the occult, then they must stop all involvement with occult activities and destroy any occult artefacts in their possession such as Ouija boards and tarot cards. Then I tell them that although they do not have to take on the Christian belief system, I will pray with them. Prayer usually provides them with relief from their anxieties – and you have to remember that only some of the people whom Jesus helped followed him in the end.'

It rapidly becomes clear when talking to Christians of a fundamentalist persuasion that they believe that someone seeking to avoid the occult will have a hard time dodging all the potential pitfalls. But such Christians do not simply pluck these pitfalls out of thin air. Instead, they point to the Bible as their guide in these as in all matters. According to Deuteronomy, Chapter 18, Verses 10 to 14:

> There shall not be found among you any one that maketh his son or his daughter to pass through the fire, or that useth divination, or an observer of times, or an enchanter, or a witch, or a charmer, or a consulter with familiar spirits, or a wizard, or a necromancer. For all that do these things are an abomination unto the Lord.

Any form of magic, including any form of fortune-telling, falls under this admonishment. Spiritualism, or spiritism such as that performed by the late Doris Stokes, also comes under attack from today's Christians who see it as involvement with the 'familiar spirits' warned about in the above passage.

Peter Anderson, an evangelist with Christian Ministries

claims: 'Of course, not every one who dabbles in spiritism becomes demon-possessed, but some do, and not always after a long and deep involvement but sometimes even with a casual and even curious investigation. You cannot know if you are susceptible, therefore leave it well alone.'

One thing the Bible does not mention is the possibility of becoming possessed through listening to rock music. But that is a belief of many of today's Christians. The bands commonly referred to by fundamentalist Christians as 'Satanic' include KISS and ACDC – which according to some Christians stand for Kids In Satanic Service and Antichrist Devil Child. These are the sorts of hugely imaginative claims that can make the unconverted look askance at the full range of such Christians' teachings. The accusations, however, continue and in 1990 the 'satanic' aspect of heavy metal was pointed up by the Cardinal of New York, John O'Connor, who predicted that heavy metal music could lead to suicide and condemned it as 'pornography in sound'. (4)

His view is echoed by the Reverend Selwyn Hughes, leader of the Surrey-based Crusade for World Renewal: 'Just as drugs can open a person to demonic activity or possession, so can certain rhythms and drummings do the same.' (5)

Tony Sarjant is another Christian who is anxious to alert people to the myriad ways in which they can become possessed by evil spirits. He and his wife Denise live in a small, picturesque village in Warwickshire. These days, Tony seems constantly bubbling over with goodwill and enthusiasm. But he recalls a life of despair – one which he devoted to the pursuit of the occult for thirty years.

As a young child, Tony suffered from polio and was in

and out of hospital for the first nine years of his life. At school he was bullied for being 'different' and he recalls how his classmates would kick him off his crutches, then run away laughing as he struggled back to his feet crying tears of frustration. A happy home life might have proved some compensation for his tormented primary school years, but Tony claims scarcely to have known his parents.

Then, when he was just ten years old, Tony discovered that he had a knack for something which would make him stand out from the crowd – not because of his disability but as someone to be admired, even revered. For the first time in his life it looked as if he could be the one holding the reins of power. This special knack he had hit upon was an ability to make the occult work for him. Other children might play with the Ouija board and levitation and nothing would happen, but when Tony presided over the lunchtime activities, things certainly did happen.

'The boys who used to jeer at me began to look up to me,' Tony recalls. 'The occult helped me to get friends – it was as simple as that. I had released a force in myself which, at the age of ten, I was quite confident I could control.' Then Tony discovered he had special psychic powers: 'I found I could use people for my own purposes, I could get them to do almost anything I wanted them to through some type of mind control I was capable of. It gave me an enormous feeling of power.' For a young disabled boy, this was heady stuff.

Tony avidly cultivated his reputation as someone with hidden powers. 'I had been forced to put up with being different since I was a child. Now I wanted to be different, I wanted people to talk about me. I had something special and people were going to respect me for it.'

Until he was sixteen, Tony traded on his reputation. He had no idea where his so-called gift came from, but he was happy to use it to his advantage. Then he began to read books about the occult, and the more he read the more fascinated he became. It seemed as if he was being offered limitless power and he would shut himself away, devouring more and more obscure works. When he did go out with his friends, they were generally up to no good, committing petty crimes such as pilfering from shops. Sometimes, one or other of his pals would get caught, but Tony claims that, nine times out of ten, he was able to use his powers to prevent himself from getting into trouble.

Every few years, however, Tony would suffer overwhelming attacks of depression.

'I was taken to see doctors and they would give me pills,' he recalls. 'I was told I was mentally ill and was put in a funny farm for two weeks. Nothing worked. I would feel better for a while, then I would suffer another attack. I would feel suicidal. Voices would tell me to kill myself. It felt as if there was a fight going on inside me but if you tell a doctor you hear voices, he automatically thinks you're crazy. They gave me pills and special diets but nothing worked. Sometimes the pills stopped me from thinking, but they were of no real use.'

Throughout the bad times, however, Tony clung on to and developed his occult powers. Somehow, he felt sure, they would guide him towards overcoming the feeling of hopelessness which threatened to engulf him. By now, Tony had begun to use the Ouija board to manifest spirits.

'Four or five of us would get together, stand around the board, and ask it questions. We saw no danger. It was amazing – we would ask it questions and we would get answers. Up until this point I had simply thought Ouija was a good laugh – I hadn't even thought about what sort of power was behind it. Then we began to conjure up spirits – you could actually see the outline of something in the room.'

It was also at around this time that Tony claims to have found he was able to predict the time and place of people's deaths. Again, his ability gave him a sense of immense power.

When he was in his early twenties, Tony met someone in a pub who knew of his fascination with the occult and asked him along to a Satanist meeting. The meetings were, says Tony, occasionally held in woods, fields and abandoned churches, but more usually in a Satanist's own home.

'The power you can get from Satanism is tremendous,' says Tony. For more than an hour, he and his fellow Satanists would worship and praise evil spirits and call on Lucifer. 'Sometimes we would manifest spirits,' he recalls. 'I would begin to feel scared at that point but I wanted the power, I wanted to get my own back on everybody who had ever upset me in any way. We all thought that Satanism would get us the good things in life.'

Soon, Tony began to suffer terrible nightmares, but his association with Satanism continued for nearly three years. By this time he was working in London as the assistant manager of a restaurant – a job he claims to have been given through Satanist contacts, though one a little less grand than the reader might have come to presume a Satanist's due.

Things came to a head when, one day, a friend of Tony's read his tarot cards:

'The cards said I had a past and a present – but they said I had no future. I was terrified. I thought I was going to

die. I realized that I had to get out of my association with
the occult – and fast.'

Overcome by an increasing sense of panic, Tony began
to look for help from any source whatsoever.

'In the end, I even tried the Church,' he says wryly.
'Eventually, a Church of England minister came to see me
with his cross, his holy water and his special prayers and
said he would exorcize me. I remember very little of the
event. The following day I knew that a powerful struggle
had taken place – the bedroom looked like a battlefield –
but I wasn't aware of what had gone on and the minister
didn't explain the exorcism to me . . . A lot of Anglican
ministers do not believe in spiritual warfare and many
churches simply refuse to speak about the subject. Not
surprisingly, they're not much use when it comes to
providing exorcisms.'

Tony clearly has little time for the Church of England.
Certainly, he considers that his exorcism at the hands of
the Church of England minister was worse than useless:

'I had come to Jesus but I hadn't cleared my past,' he
says. 'I still felt guilty about some of the things I had done.'
And he was still, he adds, troubled by evil spirits. 'Sometimes
I would feel a presence, as if something evil had just sat down
beside me. I would fall into strange inner rages and
sometimes objects would fly about the room. At night I
would suffer the most terrible dreams. For years, I was afraid
to fall asleep.' Occasionally, when he felt particularly under
attack, Tony would start praying. 'I knew when an evil spirit
was leaving me because I would begin to shiver and feel
a strange rush of cold air. I would just carry on praying,
trying to break the power of evil with something more
powerful – the power of God.'

Tony believes he was finally successfully exorcized during a praying meeting of the local fellowship church he had joined.

'Some of the guilt I felt about my past began to surface as we prayed together,' he recalls. 'We just kept praying and praying until finally I was delivered.' These days, Tony says, he is no longer troubled by fits of depression, or by nightmares. 'It's a pleasure to say that I'm not frightened by anything at all now. I know now that Jesus has the final power of victory.'

Christine Noble, a leading figure in an Essex-based fellowship church, also sees her early years as having provided fertile territory for the powers of darkness. Now in her forties, Christine was, she says, introduced to the world of the occult by her mother whom she describes as having been deeply superstitious and obsessed by the supernatural. As a young girl, Christine was taken to see fortune tellers and to seances:

'The result was that I became terribly depressed,' she says. 'I would feel afraid for no reason and would sometimes wake in the middle of the night and feel as if I was being smothered, as if I was unable to breathe. I began to think that I must be going out of my mind.'

When Christine met her husband-to-be, John Noble, he too claimed to be under the influence of demonic powers. At one time he was known as 'the ghost man' because of his ability to foretell the future and call up the past. But, like Christine, he was suffering bouts of depression and anxiety. After much discussion and soul-searching, they hit upon the idea that perhaps their occult activities had something to do with their unhappiness. Surely, they thought, there must be another side to life. Their searching brought them to the Bible where they discovered that there was a Devil as well as a God. It was their knowledge of the Devil's power that led them to Christianity.

John and Christine received no formal exorcism to rid them of the evil spirits with which they believe their years of occult involvement had landed them. Instead, the couple say they were delivered from evil through their own efforts: they prayed together and still constantly seek to 'walk in the light', convinced that if they stray from the path they will once again be open to invasion by evil spirits.

Christine sees exorcism as referring only to the ritual used to free someone from full possession.

'As a Christian, I don't believe it is possible for someone to be fully possessed; there is always a spark of the Holy Spirit within them, and so exorcism is unnecessary,' she explains. Christine does, however, think it is possible for people to be demonized and believes vehemently in the need for people to be delivered from demons.

'Demons are around us all the time,' she says, and cites the passage from Ephesians, Chapter Six: 'For we wrestle not against flesh and blood, but against principalities, against powers, against the rulers of the darkness of this world, against spiritual wickedness in high places.' Still using this passage to support her claim, she continues:

'You don't call up demons from the bowels of hell. Demons are there all the time so that when someone moves into the realm of any occult activity, such as reading tea leaves or their horoscope, the demons are there overlooking them and see a chance to move in. Sometimes a person will only be attacked by minor demons, but these lesser demons can help smooth the path for other, more dangerous ones and as you start sliding down the path it gets steeper and narrower, like a funnel.' Christine believes that 'the enemy' uses fascination and fear to attract people: 'People will often be drawn to something they don't understand – to the bizarre. But before long, the powers have trapped them.'

According to Christine, the Church of England and Catholic Church are excessively bound up with ritual. She describes them as taking the 'bell book and candle approach towards deliverance'. Instead, she believes that all Christians should be urged to discover the supernatural aspect of their faith:

'The Church isn't overt enough in pressing the fact that we serve a supernatural God. We all have a supernatural hole in us that wants to be filled, and which can be filled by God's Holy Spirit.' If the Holy Spirit gets pushed to one side, she explains, evil spirits gain entrance.

Christine and John Noble, like Roger Ellis, Tony Sarjant and Sally, belong to what is often known as the 'house church movement'. The movement earned its name from the fact that Christians, disillusioned with the mainstream Churches, would gather together in each other's homes to worship. The name 'house church movement' now seems a little inappropriate: the movement has become vast and is still growing rapidly. It is therefore more appropriate to designate members of the movement as 'New Christians'. The aim of the New Christians is to sidestep what they see as the stultifying and corrupting influence of the denominational churches and return to the form of Christian worship evident in the Early Church.

German theologian Adolf von Harnack provides an illuminating description of exorcism's place in the Early Church.

The Christians made their appearance throughout the whole world as exorcists of demons, and exorcism was a very powerful missionary and propagandist weapon. They were concerned not merely with exorcizing the demons which inhabit man, but also with purging them from the atmosphere and the whole of public life. For the century [the second] was under the dominion of the spirit of darkness and his legions . . . The whole world and the atmosphere surrounding it was peopled with devils; all the formalities of life – not only the worship of idols – were governed by them. They sat upon thrones and surrounded the infant's cradle. The earth, God's creation though it is now and for ever, became in very truth a hell. (6)

It is difficult not to notice similarities between Von Harnack's picture of the early Christians and the zeal, coupled with the dramatic worldview, of many of today's 'New Christians'. And yet, when Jesus's disciples showed excessive interest in their power to perform exorcisms, he warned them:

'Behold, I give unto you power . . . over all the power of the enemy: and nothing shall by any means hurt you. Notwithstanding in this rejoice not, that the spirits are subject unto you; but rather rejoice, because your names are written in heaven.' (7)

Although the early Christians by no means had a monopoly on exorcism, they allegedly gained a reputation for being the most powerful exorcists. According to the second-century church father, Justin Martyr, 'our Christian men . . . have healed and do heal, rendering helpless and driving the possessing devils out of the men, though they could not be cured by all the other exorcists and those who used incantations and drugs.' (8)

By the time of Origen (185–254), who is generally judged to have been the most learned and original of the Early Church Fathers, Christian exorcisms had, at least to some extent, become regulated. They were conducted free of charge and only the simplest prayers, conjurations and threats were used to banish the demon. The success of the exorcist, according to Origen, was dependent on his belief in God, and resulted from the power of the name of Jesus. Following the exorcism, the freed individual was encouraged to fast and pray.

But while Origen and other early Christians promoted a plain and simple approach towards exorcism, that approach was certainly at odds with the little we know of exorcism in Old Testament times.

In the first book of Samuel, Chapter 16, we hear how 'the Spirit of the Lord departed from Saul, and an evil spirit from the Lord troubled him.' Saul's servants decide 'to seek out a man who is a cunning player on an harp', believing that, when the harpist begins to play, Saul will be cured. All goes according to plan: the musician 'took an harp, and played with his hand: so Saul was refreshed, and was well, and the evil spirit departed from him.'

While harp-playing as a means of deliverance would probably have disturbed the austere Origen, he would almost certainly have been horrified at the razzmatazz surrounding the renowned exorcist King Solomon, who died towards the end of the tenth century BC.

King Solomon figures in occult mythology as a great magician. Such was his supernatural power that he allegedly succeeded in commanding legions of demons to build his opulent temples. Moreover, according to the first-century Jewish historian, Flavius Josephus, God enabled Solomon to learn 'the art which expels demons' and the king 'left behind him forms of exorcisms, by which people drive away demons so that they never return.' Those forms of exorcism were fashionable during the time of the early Christians.

Josephus relates the story of an exorcism he himself came across, in which the exorcist called on the power of Solomon:

'The manner of the cure was as follows: he put a ring that had under its seal one of those sorts of roots mentioned by Solomon, to the nostrils of the demoniac, and then drew the demon out through his nostrils as he smelt it: and when the man fell down immediately, he adjured the demon to return into him no more, still making mention of Solomon, and reciting the incantations which he had composed.'

Apparently, this exorcist was so determined to impress his spectators that he would place a small cup of water a short distance away from the possessed person and command the demon to overturn it when it left him or her. (9)

Today, some Christians claim that demons make their exit through a person's mouth or nose, and that they signal their departure when the afflicted person coughs or sneezes.

Some time between AD 100 and 400 a document known as the 'Testament of Solomon' appeared. It was written so that readers 'might know the powers of the demons and their forms, as well as the names of the angels by which they are thwarted'. (10) Throughout the document, there are prescriptions for the control of specific demons. According to the Testament, demons lived in precipices, caves, ravines, in the corners of houses, near the moon, among the stars and in the air. Not only did they possess men, but they would also harm them by fire, by sword – or sometimes merely by chance. Again, some of today's Christians allocate specific homes to particular demons.

Another early document advises the exorcist to 'take oil made from unripe olives, together with the plant mastigia and lotus pith, and boil it with marjoram (very colourless) saying . . . come out of this person . . .' (11) In addition, specific words and sounds were uttered during the incantations, particularly set patterns of vowels or strange words such as Ablanathanalba.

The practice of discovering the name of the demon when conducting an exorcism was also common in early times. The exorcist was advised to say: 'For I adjure you by the seal which Solomon laid upon the tongue of Jeremiah and he spake. And say whatsoever you are, in heaven, or on earth, or under the earth or below the ground . . .' (12) It is a practice continued by some exorcists to this day. These exorcists cite as their guide Mark, Chapter 5, verse 9. There, Jesus addresses the unclean spirit possessing the Gadarene demoniac, saying, 'What is thy name?' The unclean spirit answers, saying, 'My name is Legion: for we are many.'

Another method for controlling demons was by the use of amulets. According to one document, the exorcist should 'write this phylactery upon a piece of tin . . . and hang it round the sufferer: it is of every demon a thing to be trembled at, which he fears'. (13)

While many of today's Christians would frown on the superstitious flamboyance of some of these early exorcists, others appear to have woven a clutch of superstitions into the Bible's teachings on the subject. Some will go to extreme lengths in attempting to find biblical precedent for jazzing up their ministry of exorcism. American evangelist Morris

Cerrullo advises his followers to make use of what can only
be called a charm or amulet. He tells them to carry around
special prayer cloths anointed with oil which will release
them not from simply any form of bondage but specifically
from financial bondage.

Are such Christians not being drawn into the occult arts
which they so vehemently condemn? According to the
Reverend Russ Parker: 'No matter how innocent and
harmless . . . charms and amulets may appear, they are the
thin edge of the occult wedge. As such they endanger our
spiritual health and we must therefore rid ourselves of such
things.' (14)

An idea of the importance given to exorcism by the
Church Fathers is supplied by the Carthaginian theologian
Tertullian, who lived at around the same time as Origen.
He claimed that any Christian who did not know how to
exorcize demons should be put to death.

Followers of today's house church movement – or 'New
Christians' – would of course be horrified by such a
suggestion. None the less, many tend to put excessive
emphasis on demons and deliverance. The Reverend Trevor
Dearing points out that people who seem to have problems
with demons are often those who are exposed to teaching
about such entities. House churches are, he says, generally
'into' demons more than the denominations.

According to Trevor, house churches can be too extreme
and too introspective. He claims to have come across several
casualties of the movement – people who have either been
told they are infested with demons or who, on leaving the
movement, have been told that they are leaving the
Kingdom of God.

'The   nearer   the   charismatic   movement   is   to   a denominational church, the healthier it tends to be in every way – including exorcism,' says Trevor. 'Members of house churches often begin to interpret any symptoms of disquiet they might be suffering from as demon problems and come up with demons of everything under the sun.'

He cites the example of a woman who rang him up and asked to be delivered from a 'pharmaceutical demon'. 'She was taking valium and had been told by her doctor to come off gradually,' says Trevor. 'A house group told her that she was possessed by a pharmaceutical demon and that they would exorcize it from her. After performing a ritual of exorcism, the members of the house group said she could now come off the valium immediately – that there was no longer any need for her to withdraw slowly from the drug.' When the woman spoke to Trevor, she was suffering from panic attacks. Trevor advised her to go back on the valium and withdraw slowly, as her doctor had advised.

On another occasion, Trevor was contacted by a woman anxious to have the 'demon of obesity' cast out of her. A house group had told her that the cause of her weight problem was demonic. Trevor was unconvinced.

'I suggested to her that going on a diet might be a more serious approach,' he says.

Then there was the woman who contacted Trevor after having been told by a house group that she was infested by numerous demons. Members of the group claimed to cast out one demon after another from her until eventually they even cast out a 'demon of the fear of spiders'. The woman believed that from now on she would view spiders simply as another of God's friendly creatures – until she saw a specimen and screamed. In Trevor's opinion, the woman was suffering from a phobia, not a demon. The counselling she needed now was as much to help her recover from her experience with the house church as to cure her of the phobia.

Some might dismiss such goings-on as ludicrous nonsense – irresponsible, maybe, but nothing worse than that. Others would say that an excessive interest in demons and the Devil can develop into a dangerous obsession. It is a theory borne out by the tragic case of Bernadette Hasler, a young girl who in the mid-1960s was beaten to death by members of an extremist Christian group.

The group went under the disarming name of the International Family Society for the Advancement of Peace. It was founded in Germany by Magdalena Kohler and John Stocker, a defrocked priest of the Pallottine Order. Members believed that the end of the world was at hand and the organization was dominated by a sense of paranoia and fanaticism. Its founders were aided in their work by a Carmelite nun, Sister Stella, who apparently had a 'direct telephone line to heaven' and would pass on the messages she received from God to group members.

As time passed, the group gained an ever-increasing following and eventually moved to Switzerland, where it set up base on the farm of Joseph Hasler, Bernadette's father. The Hasler family soon became ardent new recruits.

More time passed, and the group's activities became increasingly bizarre. Children were taken away from their parents and raised in separate premises. Then Bernadette was told she belonged to the Devil. She herself soon began to believe it. Among the accusations levelled against her was the charge that she consorted with the Devil sexually.

The group's leaders, who by then were the only people she was allowed to see, persuaded Bernadette to make a written confession of her alleged misdeeds, and the girl complied. Her confession ran to hundreds of pages. Then began the gruelling and horrific onslaught of countless exorcisms. Twice each day, Bernadette was repeatedly beaten, a process which the group's leaders claimed would drive the Devil from her. On May 14th, 1966, she was beaten mercilessly for more than four hours. She later died. Her assailants were found guilty of causing Bernadette serious bodily harm and were sentenced to twenty years in gaol.

The list of atrocities committed with the intention of casting out the Devil goes on. A three-year-old boy was beaten to death in 1976 in the belief that he had a devil in him which needed destroying. Christian fundamentalists were involved in the killing. Four years later a baby boy, not quite two years old, was exorcised by his mother who scalded him in boiling water and then burned him to death in an oven. The woman told police that she had felt compelled to get the Devil out of her child. That same year, in Austin, Texas, a young man blew his best friend's head off with a deer rifle. He told police he had seen the Devil in his friend's head. In 1983 a two-year-old girl from California was held down by her father on a hot floor heater until, he said, the Devil left her. She died. The following year, a man from Maine burned his girlfriend's toddler to death in an oven. He claimed the four-year-old was Lucifer, and said that he had been exorcizing her.

Killings in the name of ridding the victim of the Devil or demons are not restricted to the Christian religion. In June 1991, a twenty-year-old Asian girl from Oldham, near Leeds, was beaten to death in an exorcism conducted by a Muslim 'holy man'.

The young woman, Kusor Bashir, had become

desperately depressed after failing her driving test in the spring of that year. As time passed and she showed no signs of coming out of her depression, the young woman's devout Muslim parents became convinced that their daughter was under the influence of a djinn. In Muslim lore, a djinn is a type of genie or demon who is born from fire and can bring evil and harm to human beings.

The chief 'exorcist' called in to minister to Kusor was Mohammed Bashir, a Muslim holy man known as a 'pir'. Pirs operate outside the mosques and are not recognized by the Islamic establishment. Bashir was assisted by Mohammed Nurani. The exorcists claimed that the young woman was indeed possessed by a djinn – one who went under the name of John Wayne.

For eight days, the two exorcists were guests in the home of Kusor's parents, during which time they performed their treatment. The young woman was starved of food, prevented from sleeping, forced to eat hot chilli powder and to inhale the smoke of burning mustard oil. She was also repeatedly thrashed with a walking stick.

Her parents became anxious about the methods being used but on protesting to the exorcists, they were told that their daughter felt no pain: the only being suffering was the demon. When police discovered Kusor's body, they found that fifteen of her ribs were broken, her forearms and legs were bruised and her stomach and breasts were covered in large red marks. She had also been cut across the left eye and the right breast, three times between the breasts and across the scalp. At the inquest, the pathologist said the young woman had died as a result of her ribs puncturing her lungs. These injuries were, he said, consistent with her being jumped and stamped on.

During the court case, Mr Justice McKinnon told Mohammed Bashir, 'You systematically tortured, thrashed, and finally killed the girl by breaking bones in her chest and throat in no fewer than eighteen places.'

According to many Islamic leaders, Muslims are putting increasing emphasis on the power of the djinn – just as some Christians are tending to see demons at every turn. While some pirs will charge hundreds of pounds to rid a person of an evil spirit, the true pir will never ask for payment, and will never use violence. He will simply, like the Christian exorcist, command the djinn to depart in the name of God. It is much the same form of exorcism that the early church father Origen prescribed. But it is one which, despite countless efforts, seems impossible to enforce.

The question of regulation is one which torments countless religious leaders. Today, Christians still shudder to recall the Barnsley case.

4

Enter the Professionals

The 'Barnsley case', as it has become known, took place over just a few autumn days. In that short space of time, a chain of events unfolded which led to a horrifically violent murder. It took an event like this – an exorcism which had gone tragically and frighteningly wrong – to bring the exorcism debate out into the open.

The nightmare began, seemingly innocently enough, on the night of 24th September 1974. It occurred near the town of Barnsley, Yorkshire, where thirty-one-year-old Michael Taylor lived with his twenty-nine-year-old wife, Catherine, and five sons, aged from six to twelve. That night, Michael and Catherine attended their first meeting of a local Christian fellowship group. The meeting was held in their own home at Ossett, just outside the town. Members sang hymns and someone played a guitar. Towards the end of the evening, a young woman, Marie, administered Holy Communion – despite being unordained.

A few days later, Michael went to church and in the evening a second fellowship group meeting was held at his home. During the meeting Marie began to tremble violently and then began speaking in tongues – one of the gifts of the Holy Spirit. Afterwards, she carried out a type of exorcism on a member of the group. Michael himself then suddenly began to speak in tongues himself and, trembling uncontrollably, began to wrestle with pieces of furniture.

Three days after his outburst, Michael told his mother

and two members of the fellowship group that he had seen the Devil who had instructed him to kill himself. Later that day, Marie visited him at home, and he kissed her on the lips. The following day Michael attended another fellowship meeting, this time held in Barnsley at the home of the choirmaster of St Thomas's Church, Gawber. The church's vicar, the Reverend Peter Vincent, was also present.

Michael announced to the assembled gathering that he had been seduced. It was decided that he should confess, and that a prayer of absolution should be said over him. The next day, Michael ordered his wife to rid their home of three crucifixes and various religious books. That night, he insisted on playing the radio until daybreak, saying that he was afraid of silence. The following day, a member of the fellowship group took the entire Taylor family out for a ride in his car. All of a sudden, Michael gave vent to a chilling scream, scaring the children. The driver decided to take the family to St Thomas's vicarage.

By the time they arrived, Michael's behaviour had become deranged: he was violent and noisy, hit the vicar, threw a cat through a window and splattered food on the floor. The children were put to bed upstairs and the vicar's wife suggested Michael needed exorcizing – a suggestion with which the vicar concurred.

About a mile away from St Thomas's lived methodist minister the Reverend Raymond Smith and his wife, Margaret. The couple described themselves as 'practitioners in exorcism'. The vicar's wife telephoned the Smiths and asked them to assist with Michael's case. She also called in a Methodist lay preacher from Barnsley.

By ten o'clock in the evening the six exorcists – the vicar and his wife, the Methodist minister and his wife, the

Methodist lay preacher and the member of the fellowship
group – were gathered in St Thomas's vicarage. The stage
was set to commence an all-night exorcism. By now, the
vicar's wife had come to the conclusion that Michael had
been pledged to the Devil, and that the Devil had called
on the 'power' of the moon to incite Michael to murder.
The Methodist minister, on the other hand, claimed God
had told him that Michael needed psychiatric help. The rest
of the team paid little attention to him, however, and the
Reverend Vincent announced they would go ahead with
the exorcism.

The exorcism began at about midnight. Michael was taken
to the vestry at the side of the church and laid on his back
on a pile of richly embroidered hassocks. The exorcists took
it in turn to stand over him, saying prayers and ordering
a variety of devils to be gone from him. Among the sins
which the exorcists told Michael he had committed were
those of incest and bestiality. Later, Michael insisted words
were put in his mouth.

Sins which Michael did confess to included lewdness,
blasphemy, heresy and masochism. Throughout the
operation, the exorcists repeatedly placed a wooden crucifix
in his mouth. Another wooden crucifix which Michael
himself was wearing, and which had been given to him by
Marie, was torn off him and burned in a small dish.

By this time, Michael was writhing dementedly on the
floor and the team had forcibly to hold him down. After
the exorcism, his hands were badly bruised where he had
banged them on the ground. As Michael struggled he puffed
and panted – a sign, according to the exorcists, that yet
another demon was being exorcized.

By six o'clock in the morning, the exorcists – and

Michael – were flagging. The team claimed that by this stage Michael had been rid of upwards of forty demons. After resting for an hour, the exorcists discussed their plan of action. According to the vicar's wife, Michael was still possessed by the demons of insanity, violence and murder. Nevertheless, it was decided that now was not a good time to continue with their work and so Michael was driven home. His children were sent to their grandparents and he and his wife were left alone. At 9.30 a.m. a neighbour called at the Taylors' house in Ossett. Catherine Taylor cried out: 'Don't come near me, because there is something in me.'

Half an hour later, Michael Taylor murdered his wife. Afterwards, he was found wandering the streets naked and bloodstained. He had torn his wife's face to pieces, gouging out her eyes and causing her to choke on her blood. During his trial the court heard how the murder was 'unspeakably brutal'. He was sent to Broadmoor high security prison for the criminally insane.

The case of Michael Taylor prompted a flurry of demands from Church leaders that the guidelines on exorcism should be tightened up. As it turned out, almost a decade previously the then Bishop of Exeter, the Right Reverend Robert Mortimer, had convened a commission to look into the whole area of exorcism.

The Bishop had been worried by the increasing number of people seeking help after having been involved in the occult, or having experienced poltergeist activity. It troubled him that few people in the Church of England had any knowledge or experience of exorcism. The bishop thought it was time to bring together psychiatrists, priests and theologians in order to produce a report on the subject.

The resulting booklet, *Exorcism*, was edited by the
Anglican Benedictine monk Dom Robert Petitpierre and
was published in 1972. Its aim was to act as a discussion
document and it began by setting out eight general
guidelines for dealing with people who believed themselves
to be possessed by evil spirits:

1. It cannot be overstressed that, as it is usually
   understood, the concept of demonic possession is
   extremely dubious.

2. In the first place, it should be assumed that the
   patient's illness has a physical or mental cause, and
   the case should be referred, by his general
   practitioner, to a competent physician in
   psychological medicine. The exorcism of a person
   must not be performed until possible mental or
   physical illness has been excluded in this way, and
   furthermore until a thorough investigation has
   been made of the patient in terms of spiritual
   values by a duly licensed exorcist. Only in an
   extreme emergency should either of these
   safeguards be omitted.

3. The need for exorcism, however, when all other
   steps have been taken, may still arise. The testing
   and decision about this should be undertaken
   only by a priest with experience in such matters,
   acting under the authority of the bishop of the
   diocese (and usually licensed by him for the
   work). It is not a field which forms a part of the
   ordinary duties of the pastoral ministry for which
   a parish priest may properly be assumed to be
   competent.

4. The failure of medical treatment should not necessarily be taken as evidence that the illness is spiritual . . . The diagnosis of demonic possession must rest on precise and positive criteria.

5. In every case when exorcism is decided upon, the utmost effort must be made to train the patient in the practice of Christian life . . .

6. When the patient is a Christian and a churchman, regular prayer, confession and communion should be normal. Frequent laying-on of hands and also, provided the patient is sufficiently instructed, one administration of Holy Unction are probably advisable as part of healing and may well prove to effect the cure rather than exorcism . . .

7. When the patient is not baptized, the preparation for exorcism should take the pattern of the normal preparation for baptism . . . When the patient has been baptized but is not a committed Christian, the same pattern should if possible be followed but in this case omitting baptism . . .

8. The after-care of the patient will also devolve upon the parish priest, under the guidance of the bishop or his deputy, and the importance of this work cannot be overstated. Our Lord tells us that when the evil spirit is gone out of a man the house, if left empty, will be re-occupied by evil and the last state will be worse than the first. Those who have been exorcized must be warned about this, and encouraged by all means possible to lead a prayerful life in union with the Church, to study Holy Scriptures, and to receive the sacraments regularly.

When it comes to the actual exorcism itself, the Exeter Report sets out three specific rituals from which the exorcist can choose. The first is taken from the *Rituale Romanum* which was written in 1614 on the request of Pope Paul V. The *Rituale* has remained virtually unchanged down the centuries. In particular, the *Rituale* cautioned priests against carrying out exorcisms when no true possession existed: clearly, many of the concerns troubling exorcists to this day have seen little change down the centuries either.

Two small but important revisions were made to the ritual in 1952. Previously, it had stated that symptoms of possession 'are signs of the presence of a demon'. The wording was altered to state that symptoms of possession 'might be' signs of the presence of a demon. The other revision changed the description of states other than possession from 'those who suffer from melancholia or any other illness' to 'those who suffer from illness, particularly mental illnesses'.

The principle exorcism of the ritual is interspersed with prayers and readings from the Bible. Whereas the exorcism is addressed to the demon, the prayers are addressed to the possessed individual. The ritual gets round the problem of having to be suitable for whichever demon the exorcist is dealing with by addressing every unclean spirit: 'I command you, every unclean spirit, in the Name of God the Father Almighty, in the Name of Jesus Christ his Son our Lord and our Judge, and by the power of the Holy Spirit, that you go from this image of God, whom our Lord of his goodness has called to become a temple of the living God, that the Holy Spirit may dwell in him. Through the same Christ our Lord. Amen.'

The ritual also advises exorcists as to how the exorcism should be performed and warns that most exorcisms have to be repeated over a period of days, months and sometimes even years. As well as the spoken part of the exorcism, the priest is advised to make signs of the cross, to wind his stole around the neck of the possessed person, and to perform the laying-on of hands. It is recommended that the possessed individual holds a crucifix throughout the exorcism.

Sacraments, holy water and other sacred objects such as relics are also made use of throughout the exorcism. If a woman is possessed, the exorcist is cautioned to seek the assistance of a strong woman in order to avoid any rumours of sexual misconduct. Before beginning the exorcism, the priest should make confession, then don a surplice and purple stole and commence with the ritual.

If the rite of exorcism contained in the *Rituale Romanum* is not used, the Exeter Report recommends the form of exorcism contained in the First Prayer Book of Edward VI:

> I command you, unclean spirits, in the name of the Father and of the Son and of the Holy Spirit, that you come out and depart from this person, whom our Lord Jesus Christ has vouchsafed to call to Baptism and so to be made a member of his Body and congregation. Therefore, thou cursed spirit, remember your sentence and your judgment, remember the day to be at hand wherein you shall burn in fire everlasting prepared for you and your angels. And presume not hereafter to exercise any tyranny towards this person whom Christ hath bought with his precious blood, and by his Holy Baptism called to be of his flock. (1)

The third form of exorcism referred to in the Exeter Report is taken from the East Syrian rite: 'I command you, O evil spirit, through God the Father Almighty and through Jesus

Christ his Son and through the Holy Spirit the Paraclete, that you depart, through his power, from this his vessel, whom you hold captive.'

In 1626 a *Manuale Exorcismorum* gave detailed guidelines as to how exorcisms should be carried out. It also gave numerous formulae for the rites, one covering almost forty pages. According to the Manual, the exorcist's most powerful tool in overcoming the Devil is his own faith in God and Jesus. Before conducting the exorcism, the exorcist is advised to prepare himself inwardly by fasting and prayer. The Manual recommends that the exorcism should be carried out in a church, or some other place consecrated to God. Only in an emergency should the exorcism take place in a private house. Much of the advice found in the *Manuale Exorcismorum* and the *Rituale Romanum* is included in the Exeter Report's fifteen recommendations for 'The Exorcism and Blessing of a Person':

1. The priest should only undertake the exorcism of a person if he himself is in a state of recollection and confident of our Lord's victory over evil in general and in the situation confronting him.

2. It is wise to share such situations with another priest experienced in this aspect of the ministry.

3. The priest should prepare himself and those present by confession, prayer and fasting, and if possible communion together.

4. Those present should consist only of mature Christian people who are sympathetic to this ministry.

5. People unknown to the priest should not be

present. This includes those 'interested' – reporters, and so on, not least because of the spiritual danger in which they place themselves.

6. If the exorcism takes place in a house, animals and children should be removed, and the latter given a prayer of protection and a blessing before the service begins.

7. The service should, if possible, take place in a church, or at least in a place chosen by or agreeable to the exorcist.

8. Appropriate steps should be taken to ensure that no unscheduled exit on the part of the person is possible before the ministration is complete.

9. It is recommended that doctors and psychiatrists are aware of the steps being taken and that they are invited to attend.

10. Prayers of a select number of other Christians not present should be encouraged, not only for the sufferer but also for those present and the exorcist. Such imparted knowledge need not include personal details, and must not be such as would break confidences or cause gossip.

11. As, occasionally, a prolonged period is necessary, two hours or more should be made available so that if the case is of this nature the person will not be left in a state of acute distress by an incompleted ministry.

12. If the sufferer is brought into church, he should on no account be left alone, but at least two people, capable of restraining violent activity, should stay with him. (If these people are to attend the exorcism itself, it will mean that

separate arrangements may have to be made for their spiritual preparation.)

13. The priest should not hesitate at any time prior to the exorcism itself to dismiss any person or persons whose presence, for any reason, he feels to be inappropriate. The presence of another priest makes it possible for the would-be exorcist, if inexperienced, to exclude himself should he, for example, experience sudden doubt or fear. This is not a trivial point.

14. Because of the possibility of self-injury, the patient could well be seated in a deep armchair throughout the service.

15. The exorcist should be open to the possibility that after the exorcism other sacramental means of grace would be appropriate: e.g. Holy Communion, Holy Unction, and perhaps even Baptism. It is wise to arrange things so that these are readily available without the need for extensive preparations.

The exorcism of Michael Taylor had broken two of the cardinal guidelines laid down in the Exeter report: the 'Barnsley six' exorcists had not sought medical opinion before carrying out the exorcism, and they had not completed the exorcism.

But there was no reason why the Barnsley six exorcists should have consulted the report. Although it had been published two years earlier, it had no official status: priests with a particular interest in exorcism may have read it, but the recommendations made by the report were not officially implemented.

It took the tragedy of the Barnsley case to stir up interest in exorcism and bring the debate out into the open. But by no means everyone considered that laying down guidelines for exorcism was a good thing.

One line of thought was represented by the Reverend Don Cupitt, Dean of Emmanuel College, Cambridge. In May 1975 he helped organize an open letter to the Archbishops of Canterbury and of York, and all bishops and members of the General Synod. The letter was aimed at influencing that July's General Synod debate on the matter.

Among the letter's sixty-five signatories were thirteen theology professors, five Anglican theological college principals, and the then Bishop of St Albans, the Right Reverend Robert Runcie, later to become Archbishop of Canterbury. The letter's signatories were at pains to make it clear that:

> We believe that the Church of England is in danger of making a serious error of judgment. For some years now the practice of exorcism has been growing, with some encouragement from the authorities, in many English dioceses . . . Our fear is that, since exorcism has already come to be widely practised, a compromise will be worked out. To control its excesses, exorcism will be regulated: but the effect of this will be to give it more nearly official status in the Church than it has had since the old baptismal exorcism was abolished in 1552. We believe that exorcism should have no official status in the Church at all . . .

The letter claimed that exorcism was at variance with the entire history and tradition of the Church of England. It pointed to the danger of encouraging belief in occult evil powers capable of depriving men of their normal moral responsibility. And it claimed that, since the Reformation and the rise of modern science, mankind had been liberated from demonological and similar beliefs. The proper way to cast out evil, according to the letter's signatories, was by repentance, faith, prayer and the sacraments. While recognizing that Jesus had performed exorcisms, the letter said that the Church had never expected that her members should share all of Jesus's beliefs.

In conclusion, the letter's signatories claimed that:

> It is, we think, mistaken to suppose that loyalty to Christ requires the Church to re-create, in late twentieth-century Europe, the outlook and practices of first-century Palestine. Such an attempt invites ridicule, not to mention the harm that may be done. We urge all who hold high office in the Church to ensure that the practice of exorcism receives no official encouragement and gains no official status in the Church. (2)

It was a point of view echoed by the Right Reverend David Brown, Bishop of Guildford, who wrote in his diocesan newsletter:

> Some would say that our Lord cast out demons and that his ministers should do the same. This can be a real difficulty if we give this kind of ministry a prominent place in the life of the Church. Our Lord, however, spoke in a way that was appropriate to his contemporaries. In his human life he was subject to the limitations of human existence and the extent of his knowledge was that of

a man of his own time. Medical science, including psychology and the study of mental disorders, has greatly advanced since his time and it is not always appropriate to use his language.

And according to the Reverend Michael Wilson, a doctor and also senior lecturer in pastoral theology at Birmingham University:

I personally feel under no pressure to believe in possession by evil spirits just because Jesus believed in them. I feel under no obligation to exorcize anyone simply because Jesus and his contemporaries did so. The reason I feel free in this regard is because I believe in the incarnation. Jesus was born a Jew in Bethlehem when Cyrenius was Governor in Syria. He really was made flesh and partook of the family, social and religious life of his day. A great deal of disturbed behaviour was then perceived as if caused by possession. It was the usual way to perceive it in those days, in that culture. I have little doubt that Jesus also believed the world was flat. That too, was the usual belief of his day. That is what for me it means that Jesus was true man–God accepting limitations of first-century Jewish flesh and knowledge.

In July 1975, the House of Bishops, as if treading on eggshells, laid down cautious guidelines on exorcism at the General Synod. The ruling was:

. . . there are many men and women so within the grip of the power of evil that they need the aid of the Christian Church in delivering them from it. When this ministry

is carried out the following factors should be borne in
mind:

1. It should be done in collaboration with the
   resources of medicine.
2. It should be done in the context of prayer and
   sacrament.
3. It should be done with the minimum of publicity.
4. It should be done by experienced persons
   authorized by the diocesan bishop.
5. It should be followed up by continuing pastoral
   care. (3)

The Church of England was not alone in finally speaking
out on the subject of exorcism. The following year, the
Methodist Conference, also prompted by the wave of
concern about exorcism caused by the Barnsley case,
approved a *Statement on Exorcism* which noted three different
views.

One was that 'The process of exorcism involved the
casting out of an objective power of evil which has gained
possession of a person. This view includes the conviction
that the authority to exorcize has been given to the Church
as one of the ways in which Christ's Ministry is continued
in the world.'

The second view was that 'The process of exorcism is
a necessary or at least an effective psychological means of
reassuring those who believe themselves to be possessed'
and that as a result 'pastoral responsibility involves acceptance
of the frame of reference of the person who seeks help.'

The third view was that 'A belief in demons is explicable
sociologically and psychologically. It is undeniable that

there are people who claim to believe in demons, but – since demons do not exist – it is their belief with which we should deal, not demons, In this case exorcism would be inappropriate, since what is to be dealt with is false belief.'

It was this third view that the Church of Scotland adhered to in its *Report of the Working Party on Parapsychology*, issued in May 1976. The report concluded:

> . . . such a ceremonial as Exorcism does more harm than good by its existence within the practice of the Church. We believe that it affects nothing that cannot be accomplished by expeditious use of medical skills, the latter including prayer, blessing and such healing procedures as the pastoral agent may have at his disposal.
>
> A special ceremonial designed to expel evil spirits must tend to produce a misunderstanding of the role of the pastor which seems to give him magic powers . . . In accordance with this conclusion, the Working Party must recommend that ministers of the Church of Scotland should be enjoined to refrain from conducting a special ceremony of Exorcism. The concomitant of this must be that we are of the opinion that any person encountering a case of 'alleged possession' should refer it to a physician and remain in consultation with him as to treatment thereafter.

While the report included an escape clause, allowing exorcism to be an appropriate method of treatment 'in the most exceptional circumstances', in 1985 the Church of Scotland underlined its rejection of exorcism. That year, it released another report which said that exorcism ceremonies appeared to create unjustified belief, anxiety and hysteria about demons or a devil. The report, drawn up by five ministers and three laymen, commended Martin Luther's remedy of hurling an ink pot at the Devil as more useful than spilling its own rivers of ink in 'serious and laborious inquiry into the diabolic or demonic'. (4)

But while the Church of Scotland all but rejected the practice of exorcism, the Church of England has continued to devote a good deal of attention to the issue. The commission convened by the Bishop of Exeter developed into the Christian Exorcism Study Group, later renamed the Christian Deliverance Study Group. The new name was chosen in order to deflect any sensationalism associated with the word exorcism and to reflect the group's aim to widen its scope and also help those not requiring a full-blown exorcism.

These days, each diocese in the Church of England has its team of exorcists, sometimes numbering up to six and including medical advisers as well as priests. The teams also tend to have at least one female member. The thinking behind this is the same as that put forward in the *Manuale Exorcismorum*: that if a male priest were left to deal with a possessed woman, accusations of sexual misconduct might arise. The presence of at least one other woman will, it is hoped, firmly quash any such rumours.

The decision as to who should act as diocesan adviser on exorcism is made by the diocesan bishop. He will take into account the priest's experience and training, but will pay particular attention to his personal qualities. In his book *Hostage to the Devil* (1976), the former Jesuit professor Dr Malachi Martin lists the qualities he judges to be appropriate:

Usually he is engaged in the active ministry of parishes. Rarely is he a scholarly type engaged in teaching or research. Rarely is he a recently ordained priest. If there is any median age for exorcists, it is probably between the ages of fifty and sixty-five. Sound and robust physical health is not a characteristic of exorcists, nor is proven intellectual brilliance, postgraduate degrees, even in psychology or philosophy, or a very sophisticated personal culture . . . Though, of course, there are many exceptions, the usual reasons for a priest's being chosen are his qualities of moral judgment, personal behaviour, and religious beliefs – qualities that are not sophisticated or laboriously acquired, but that somehow seem always to have been an easy and natural part of such a man.

Each year the Christian Deliverance Study Group runs a training course for those called on to help out in the field of exorcism. The course is usually held in a retreat centre not far from Leamington Spa in Warwickshire (which just happens to be the birthplace of the renowned occultist Aleister Crowley). It lasts four days and is attended by about thirty newcomers to the field. Two psychiatrists and two priests with experience of exorcism talk to the newcomers about their work and advise them on how to recognize the symptoms of possession. Although most of those who sign up for the Study Group's training are Anglicans, people of other denominations, including Roman Catholic priests, also attend the course.

The Study Group offers practical advice to Christians faced with someone in need of deliverance. Among its many recommendations, it suggests that they should not attempt to tackle the problem alone and that, as well as bringing in a Christian friend or group, they should ask Christian communities to pray for them. The group also stresses the vital need for aftercare.

According to the group a number of dangers may confront the 'counsellor' (the title used to describe the person conducting the deliverance or exorcism). The principal spiritual dangers are judged to be 'concentration on self and residual doubt of God's authority'. Counsellors are warned not to become filled with personal self-confidence since it is God's power which enables them to cast out spirits. They should also beware of doubting God's power: He will deal with the given situation in His own way – which might not necessarily be that which the exorcist had in mind.

Counsellors are also warned not to become excessively absorbed by or fascinated with evil. According to the group, 'It is dangerous to enthrone the powers of evil, and easy to accept the idea of a majestic, dark god of Evil, or of a beautiful fallen angel of Mephistophelean proportions.' They are also advised to 'Beware of finding demons because you are looking for them, or because the client believes they are involved. Beware of putting people into standard categories derived from the last case you were involved in. Beware of setting up as an amateur psychiatrist or doctor, rather than putting the skills of your own disciplines into the service of theirs if they should require it. Always go for the simplest answer that will explain what is going on, rather than the more complex one, even though you know that complexities may well arise.'

Another alleged danger to the counsellor comes in the form of psychical attacks from Satanists. However, the group offers reassurance in claiming that only those Christians who are relying on their own power rather than that of Christ will really be under threat. Counsellors can also draw reassurance from Jesus's promise to his disciples in St Luke's gospel: 'Behold, I give unto you power to tread on serpents and scorpions, and over all the power of the enemy: and nothing shall by any means hurt you.' (5)

Canon Dominic Walker is co-chairman of the Christian Deliverance Study Group. His long standing in the field of exorcism has earned him the title of chief exorcist to the Church of England. While radiating good humour and health, he is also an imposing figure in his black clerical garb and with his black hair, elegantly peppered with white.

Canon Walker admits to having been a little wary of the Study Group before first attending one of its meetings.

'When I finally met the members, I was relieved to discover how sane they were,' he recalls. 'They actually agreed with me on many key issues. I was surprised how open-minded they were.' He has, however, been attacked by evangelicals for his views.

'They say that I don't have a fundamentalist understanding of Christianity,' he explains. 'I, however, believe that our task is to interpret the truths of the Bible for the twentieth century.'

Just a few years after his ordination, while working in the diocese of Southwark, London, Canon Walker's bishop asked him to take on the task of advising him on the ministry of exorcism. The bishop chose the young priest for this particular line of work, knowing of his long-standing interest in psychology. It was an interest which had already prompted Canon Walker to undergo training in Jungian therapy, and Jungian analysis continues to colour his approach towards the area of deliverance.

Now Vicar of Brighton, Canon Walker takes what he

describes as a holistic view of any case of alleged possession he comes across.

'We suffer from the idea that we are divided into three parts – body, mind and soul, and that each part comes solely under the care of the GP, psychiatrist or priest,' he says. 'We should, however, be ministering to all these different aspects of the individual.'

The more cases of possession Canon Walker encounters, the more, he says, he is convinced that the problem must be dealt with as resulting from a lack of harmony, or holism, within the individual:

'Increasingly, I feel that devils are the unhealed part of a person's unconscious and that what, as an exorcist, I do is to bring this to the surface. Exorcism is, I think, a unique form of healing.'

Unhealed parts of the unconscious can, in Canon Walker's experience, be extremely dangerous. He sees the Ouija board as just one method of getting in touch with this unhealed aspect of the self.

'I remember a girl who was devastated after being jilted by her boyfriend,' he explains. 'Her friends invited her round for a drink and, after they'd had a few, they brought out the Ouija board. The message relayed to the girl was that no man would ever love her. The next day, she threw herself off a tower block.'

The first time Canon Walker came across someone whom he himself thought was possessed was when he was called in to see a twenty-two-year-old woman in a psychiatric clinic. The woman had not responded to any psychotherapy or drugs and was totally convinced she was possessed. She claimed she had given her life to Satan because God had failed to do anything for her.

Before being admitted to a psychiatric hospital, the woman had been involved with a charismatic group of Christians for about a year. As far as Canon Walker could establish, the group had been using her as a scapegoat for their problems and, after projecting their problems onto her, had attempted to exorcize her. 'They actually tried to kick the devil out of her – physically,' he says.

'I watched her being interviewed by two psychiatrists, and then I interviewed her myself,' Canon Walker recalls. 'Then, since nothing else was working, we decided that it was worth attempting an exorcism. When we carried out the exorcism she behaved in a very bizarre fashion and spoke in the voices of three different people – all of them men. One of the voices was Death, one Envy and one Lust. Then the woman's face contorted and she threw herself to the ground and hissed like a snake. I had taken my kit with me – including holy water and a crucifix – and when I sprinkled her with the water, it left a mark on her skin.'

Canon Walker began by casting Death out of the young woman, then moved on to Envy and Lust. He recalls how, having finished, the first voice returned saying, 'I am back you bastard'.

'At this point I remember telling myself "You mustn't stop. You must go on until you win". I told the voice that Death was no more, that Christ had overcome death. It felt as if the whole exorcism lasted for ages but in fact it only took about twenty minutes,' he continues. 'Eventually the woman collapsed, and when she came to she was OK.'

These days, Canon Walker believes that the voices issuing from the woman were all manifestations of aspects of her inner self that needed to be healed. His attitude at the time was, however, different:

'At that stage, fifteen years ago, I thought that I was dealing with what appeared to be a demon. I would still refer to these things as demons, but now I see demons as being part of us and Satan as being the dark side of the human psyche. You have to get people to own their own demons and own their own poltergeists.'

Despite such a psychologically based understanding of possession, Canon Walker has come across characteristics of the condition which appear to defy logical explanation. As with his experience of poltergeists, he now believes that the human psyche is capable of phenomena of which as yet we only have the merest glimmerings of comprehension.

He cites as an example two cases of possession he has dealt with in which the possessed individual has spoken fluently in a language of which they have absolutely no knowledge. One case was that of a man in a psychiatric hospital who had been diagnosed as having possession syndrome – the belief that he was possessed. The man – who had, says Canon Walker, never laid foot outside Britain – had a background of occult involvement. The psychiatrists called in Canon Walker as a last resort.

'I started saying prayers of exorcism over him and he suddenly began to speak in Arabic, he recalls. 'We weren't sure what language it was until we called in an Egyptian doctor who was able to have a conversation with him.' After the exorcism, the man recovered and had no memory of his brief linguistic ability.

The other case was of an Englishwoman who broke into fluent Norwegian despite having no previous knowledge of the language. Canon Walker insists that in both cases, the person concerned could not have learnt the language unconsciously – for instance by listening to neighbours speaking it for hour upon hour and so soaking it up. What he does think possible is that the person had, under pressure, tapped into the 'collective unconscious', a Jungian term for the past experience of the human species which, according to Jung, has been built into the inherited brain structure.

Canon Walker will also use his expertise as an exorcist to minister to those suffering from physical ailments. But he believes that seeing illness as a demon is unhelpful and all too often simply provides an excuse for laying the blame on something else and evading responsibility. He recounts the case of a mother who brought her nine-year-old daughter to him, convinced she was suffering from a demon of bed-wetting – a diagnosis she had been given by members of her house church:

'I sent the mother out of the room and the little girl burst into tears and said she was unhappy because she had been put up a class at school. That, not demons, was clearly the root of the problem.'

Another case Canon Walker dealt with was that of an Indian baby who was blind in one eye, and then at eighteen months lost the sight in the other. The baby's parents visited countless experts, none of whom was able to help. Eventually they brought their child to a top ophthalmologist in London. He suggested they try unconventional means of curing their child and the couple turned for help to a doctor and former missionary. According to Canon Walker, the doctor suffers from 'a real hang-up about aborted and unwanted children', even describing them as carrying on growing and 'playing football with the guardian angels'.

'None the less,' says Canon Walker, 'he does have visions which give him some very deep insights into people he is ministering to. But while his therapeutic approach might be very good, his theology implies that God is either cruel or limited if there are all these aborted souls wandering around attacking living souls.'

According to Canon Walker, 'The doctor said that the baby was blind because its grandmother had had an abortion and that the aborted child was trying to stop the living child from seeing. I felt that the reason could be that the child was suffering from hysterical blindness and had chosen not to see, or that the parents didn't want the child to see them because they felt ashamed of something. All the same, the parents would desperately try to stimulate their child to see with coloured flashing lights and so they certainly weren't consciously trying to prevent it from seeing.'

Following the doctor's instructions, a requiem mass was held for the aborted child of the grandmother.

'Then I let the parents pray,' Canon Walker recalls. 'They wept profusely. The whole history of their guilt came out – guilt that the grandmother had aborted her child and that the family had refused to confront the matter, and also guilt about other matters which hadn't been cleared up. I anointed the baby with oil and the couple went back to India. A year later, the father called me up and said that from the moment they had received deliverance, the child's sight had begun to come back. At the time he spoke to me, it had recovered ninety-five per cent vision in one eye.'

While the approach Anglicans take towards the ministry of deliverance can vary to a huge degree, they do at any rate have guidelines to which they can refer. They are also to some degree accountable for the action they take and are supposed to seek advice on deliverance from their diocesan team of exorcists and permission to perform an exorcism from their diocesan bishop. The Reverend Trevor Dearing is, however, just one of several Anglican exorcists who says that many cases of demonic possession have to be dealt with instantly, and that it is ludicrous, and dangerous, to wait to seek approval from the bishop before carrying them out.

However, ministers of denominations which provide no guidelines on exorcism can feel virtually stranded when they encounter people in need of deliverance.

While the Church of England was hammering out its guidelines on exorcism, a Baptist pastor in the north of England was undergoing his introduction to the world of the occult.

'All I was aware of in the early seventies was the odd book in which Christians described their past experiences in the occult,' says Nigel Wright, now a lecturer at Spurgeon's College, a Baptist training centre in south London. 'I thought what they were writing about was totally bizarre. Then, I was thrown in at the deep end and encountered the occult myself.'

Nigel has since helped to teach many trainee pastors about the field of deliverance and also advises the Baptist Union on deliverance and exorcism. Although he has argued that there should be an advisory group on deliverance for the Baptist Union, his suggestion has so far been rejected.

'We can't insist people have advice, but we can offer it,' says Nigel. 'An advisory group would enable us to introduce some form of accountability to the field of deliverance, it would enable us to prevent mistakes from happening – and it would mean that Baptists didn't have to invent the wheel every time they came across someone in need of deliverance.'

Certainly, it seems that Baptist pastors are in need of some form of advice where deliverance is concerned: a study of students who had left Spurgeon's over a five-year period showed that every one of them had encountered cases of apparent demonization after leaving the college.

Nigel's introduction to the area happened quite by chance:

'People from all sorts of backgrounds began coming to me and relating their experience of things I simply didn't know how to interpret,' he recalls. 'One girl, a non-Christian who was into Blackpool's nightclub culture, described a spirit that appeared to her as a Nazi SS officer and would force her to have sex with him. We prayed for her on several occasions and eventually she stopped coming to me.'

Following this experience, Nigel was left wondering how to come to an understanding of what the girl had told him. Was she suffering from some strange psychosis? Was she really experiencing this phenomenon? Or was she simply imagining things? Nigel has no easy answers and admits that at the end of the day, he is an agnostic about what is actually happening to the person who claims to be, or appears to be, possessed.

'It is still a mystery as to what we are dealing with,' he says.

On several occasions, however, he has been convinced that people who have approached him seeking deliverance have simply been fantasizing about their pasts.

'They would say, for instance, that the doctor who had delivered them at their birth was a Satanist,' he says. 'I suspected that these people were under severe stress and, having been pushed beyond a certain point, were dredging up the most fantastic things from the subconscious as a way of explaining what they were going through.'

One of the first cases Nigel encountered was that of a woman in her forties who was coming out of Mormonism.

'She was passed on to me by people who thought they had delivered her but when she came to me, more things began to emerge,' he recalls. 'She was clearly tormented and I tried to identify what it was that was troubling her. Sometimes, I could make no more than an inspired guess. I would pray over her for about fifteen minutes and tell whatever it was to go in the name of Jesus. Then something else would pop up – it was like a box of tissues. In this case, it took about a year before all the "demons" had disappeared. I just had to respond to whatever popped up next. In the end, she was totally free of all these things, but she was still a damaged person who needed love, care and support and we had to ensure that she received that kind of help.'

Before encountering this woman, Nigel admits that he was a sceptic as far as demonic possession was concerned. Afterwards, he went through a significant shift in his thinking. But he still struggles to understand exactly what it is that is causing such distress to his clients.

'Up until then I had of course read about the category of the satanic and demonic in the New Testament but that was it,' he admits. He has now come to the conclusion that evil is not an ordered system.

'Whereas some of those in the deliverance ministry see evil as a very precise system with a chief devil at the top and a hierarchy of lesser demons underneath him, I tend to see evil as chaotic,' he explains. 'Maybe it helps people to see evil as an ordered hierarchy but I am sure that in doing so they fail to deal with many other aspects of deliverance. Besides, if you take it that evil is chaos and deceptive, demons must quite enjoy all this. They must take delight in confusing people.'

Through these and other experiences, Nigel began to formulate his own approach to dealing with the growing number of people who came to him for help.

'I realized that a mature deliverance ministry would look for explanations other than demonization for most of the phenomena encountered and would relegate the category of the demonic to only one part of that ministry,' he explains.

As a result of his line of thinking, Nigel will spend several hours counselling someone who appears to be possessed before praying over them. 'In this way, I can determine what their needs are and can help them to take responsibility for their own lives and own problems,' he says.

Nigel has, however, come to the conclusion that deliverance not only benefits those who truly appear 'demonized' but that it can also solve non-demonic problems.

'I see deliverance as covering a fairly broad spectrum,' he explains. 'It is not an exact science and sometimes a deliverance mode seems to be the only thing that will help people, even though they might not be "demonized" as it is generally understood. For instance, it might emerge during a counselling session that a person is imprisoned by their past life, or by their childhood rather than by demons. Christians have the authority to set people free whatever they are suffering from.'

Through counselling, Nigel aims to find out about the person he is dealing with and to discover how evil has entered their life.

'You have to find out what it is about this person that has allowed them to become distorted by evil, in what way the powers of darkness have affected them. It is important to concentrate on the person you are dealing with, not on the demon. Deliverance should, above all, be person-centred,' he insists.

Nigel is likely to suspect that a person is indeed demonized if he feels that he or she is in the power of some other being.

'If someone is behaving in a way beyond their own potential, then it can at any rate be useful to deal with that person as if they are possessed,' he explains. 'According to received wisdom, the way to deal with that person is to isolate the aspect of them which appears to be causing the trouble and ask it to reveal itself, to say its name. In response, they might say, "I am the demon of lust" or "I am the demon of desire". Whether or not this is a demon or whether it is a parasitical negative thought plaguing the person, I cannot be certain. It may, of course, be both – evil might take the form of a parasitical thought.'

One of the first lessons Nigel had to learn was what it meant to have authority in the name of Christ, to have the ability, through Christ, to cast out evil.

'I knew Christ's power was superior to the powers of darkness – but that also presented problems since I had to be aware of the danger of becoming arrogant. I had constantly to remind myself that it is possible to abuse power.'

None the less, that power has often come to his aid – not only when dealing with other people.

'In the early days I would sometimes wake up in the middle of the night feeling very afraid and as if I was being attacked by something,' he recalls. 'I found, however, that if I thought of Christ and took authority in his name over whatever it was, then I would immediately relax.'

Nigel has also been attacked by the people he has been ministering to. In the middle of a prayer they might suddenly lash out as if seeking to destroy him. On other occasions, they will twist, gyrate and retch – and their faces will become horribly distorted.

'In situations like this it is obvious that these people are in the grip of something bigger than themselves,' he says.

When Nigel told the staff at Spurgeon's of the strange, sometimes terrifying, phenomena he had encountered, he was met with disbelief.

'Although I could understand their attitude, I had genuine coal-face experience,' he insists. 'I had definite, concrete experience of what I was telling them about. I was not simply fantasizing.'

He now makes it his task to ensure that he is always available to advise the college students on how to deal with cases of apparent possession.

Much of the advice Nigel offers comes in the form of down-to-earth common sense. He says, for instance, that it is best never to conduct a deliverance when children are around – not because the children are likely to 'catch' the demon but simply because they could become frightened by the noise. He also advises people to conduct the deliverance in a church building. Again, this is not because a church building has some form of magic power over demons, but because it is likely to be a peaceful place where the presence of God can be felt.

One warning he offers is that a deliverance should never be conducted late at night – not because ghouls are likely to creep out of the woodwork come midnight but because the strength of those involved in the deliverance will be sapped. For the same reason, he suggests that the deliverance should never last for longer than two hours in one session.

Nigel stresses that it is important not to allow the client, or the demons, to determine the agenda. Instead, he says that the person conducting the deliverance should make it clear from the outset that he is in charge of the proceedings.

'It is also important for the person conducting the deliverance to have someone there with him with whom he can check what has actually been going on, to keep him in touch with reality,' he continues. 'Also, if they are praying for a woman, they should make sure another woman is there, simply because of the sexual dangers,' he adds.

And then comes the piece of advice which is perhaps hardest for those new to the deliverance ministry to follow. It is, Nigel insists, extremely important to maintain a critical distance from what is going on. Otherwise, the person conducting the deliverance can lose perspective and become obsessed by evil.

As for the actual process of deliverance, Nigel considers that after being counselled, the person conducting the deliverance should tell his client what he is going to do and ask what they themselves expect to happen. The client must then demonstrate repentance for whatever it is that is at the root of the problem, and must then renounce that evil.

'Only then,' says Nigel, 'do you break the power holding them in the name of Jesus Christ: It is the authority of Christ that is the important fact. The person then needs healing, restoration and counselling.'

Even if the utmost care is taken, says Nigel, the deliverance might not be effective and might need to be repeated over a long period of time.

'Deliverance is never simple. Sometimes the person conducting it doesn't have enough authority or sometimes the demons have embedded themselves so deeply that it takes a long time to root them out. It might also be that the client is hanging on to his or her past ways of living, that they don't really want to be free.'

Nigel himself has occasionally felt that he has failed to help people seeking deliverance.

'In one situation, there was a member of our church who received quite a lot of deliverance ministry,' he recalls. 'It got to the point when we would pray with him and he would respond in certain set ways. We began to feel we were failing him but eventually we came to the conclusion that we had genuinely delivered him of a number of things but that he then got into an autonomic, self-perpetuating form of response to our ministry. We had to say to him, "Actually, you're fine, there is nothing else for you to be free from".'

Looking back over his years in the deliverance ministry, Nigel finds it hard to explain why he was called to this particular line of work.

'Some people will never encounter people in need of deliverance,' he says. 'One possible explanation for this is that demonization only comes to light in certain situations, and in the presence of certain people. Having been thrust into this realm, I believe I have developed a capacity to expose it, to bring it to the light. Often I can look at a person and get the feeling that something needs sorting out, just by spending time with them. Of course, this doesn't necessarily mean that the person is demonized – that could lead to witch-hunts. But I have come to trust myself to be correct.'

He ends on a note of caution.

'A lady once came up to me and said, "Nigel, I have the gift of discernment." I was immediately sceptical. Discernment is not a gift that you carry around. I can be discerning. I can be obtuse. None the less, though they are not infallible, some people have a gift which enables them to be particularly effective in the area of deliverance.'

The test of time, and the testament of the countless people he has delivered has, according to Nigel Wright, proved him one of them.

5

Things That Go Bump

For years, the Reverend Dr Donald Omand was known as one of the world's leading exorcists. Born in 1903, his first calling was to journalism and it was in his capacity as a reporter that he met Gestapo chief Heinrich Himmler in 1934. The encounter persuaded him of the reality of evil and in 1951 he became a Church of England minister. But it was the presence of evil in places rather than in people which most troubled Omand.

He became convinced that certain stretches of land and sea were inhabited by evil spirits and travelled throughout the globe tracking down these death traps. One of his forays took him to an area of sea north of the Arctic Circle where Norwegian sailors had succumbed to what is known as 'sea madness' – a compulsion to throw themselves overboard and drown. In this area, sea madness was believed to affect only those people with Viking ancestry. During the exorcism, Omand too felt drawn to fling himself into the sea. It was only after the event that he recalled that he himself was of Viking descent.

The most notorious exorcism Omand conducted was that of the Bermuda Triangle, the stretch of sea covering some one and a half million square miles where numerous ships and aircraft have disappeared without trace. According to Omand, the evil lurking within the Triangle was a result of the agony of West Africans who had died within its boundaries while they were being shipped to America as slaves.

Areas infested by evil spirits were, according to Omand, not always on so grand a scale. He developed the theory that so-called black spots on roads, where motorists repeatedly have accidents, are also the domain of malign entities. After interviewing numerous accident victims, he discovered that at these particular places drivers, far from losing control on a tricky bend, had actually felt compelled to crash their vehicles.

As a result of this discovery, Omand devoted much of his time to exorcizing roads and was sometimes called on by particular policemen to carry out the ritual.

The Reverend Tom Willis, Vicar of Holy Trinity Church in Sowerby, Yorkshire, has also repeatedly been called on to exorcize places. His most notorious case occurred in the late 1980s and was that of a trawler, the *Pickering*, which the crew claimed was haunted by a supernatural being. Whenever the ship put out to sea, its steering went haywire and the engine time and again broke down. Even when the ship's heating was turned full on, the cabins remained freezing and its lights would flicker eerily on and off. One member of the crew even reported seeing a ghostly figure which sported a flat cap stalking the deck.

The *Pickering*'s crew of five were so disturbed by these phenomena that they refused to put out to sea and so were forced to claim benefits. Eventually, the Department of Health and Social Security was alerted to the situation and, convinced the men were telling the truth, called in the Reverend Willis to exorcize the ship.

Reverend Willis conducted some detailed research into the ship's past history and discovered that a deckhand had once been washed overboard. As far as the minister could ascertain, it seemed likely that it was the deckhand's spirit that was haunting the trawler. As a result, he sprinkled the ship with holy water, led prayers and told the spirit to depart, whereupon the trouble ceased and the crew went back to work.

According to the Reverend Michael Perry, Archdeacon of Durham, many apparent hauntings are in fact place memories. These are, he explains:

> . . . memories which have become attached to places in the past in such a way that they can be reactivated and replayed in the present. In themselves they are neither good nor evil, and are impersonal. They show no sign of intelligence, nor do they recognize or react to the persons who observe them. Frequently they simply mechanically repeat a particular action, or walk over a particular route, and disappear when they have completed it – as though they were no more than 'video–clips', not the real persons of whom the clips are images. (1)

The idea that ghosts are in fact simply recordings of events that have taken place in the past has been explored by numerous investigators including the psychic T. C. Lethbridge. He, like Michael Perry, put forward the idea that if something unpleasant had occurred at a particular place, it left behind some form of trace. Lethbridge, however, believed that the trace memory was stored in a type of recording medium such as the electrical field of an area of water.

Sometimes, the place memory will lie dormant for decades, even centuries. It will be reactivated by, for example, a similar incident in the present or by a particular person who tunes in to the past occurrence. This person will occasionally pass the place memory on to other people by some form of telepathy and so they, too, think they have seen the 'ghost'.

In time, however, place memories fade out, becoming increasingly indistinct and confused. A place memory can be distinguished from a true haunting by its repetitiveness.

Dom Robert Petitpierre, author of the Bishop of Exeter's report on exorcism, was once contacted by a family troubled by the fact that, each full moon, the apparition of a stag, followed by huntsmen and a pack of hounds, would plough through their billiard room. Petitpierre told the family that the apparition was harmless and that there was little they could do to prevent its appearance. He did, however, add that sometimes the apparition could be closed out by altering the dimensions of a room. The family followed his advice and raised the billiard room's floor level. The next full moon, they looked on horrified as the head of a stag, followed by horses' heads and huntsmen's torsos charged through their billiard room.

Michael Perry believes that place memories do not need to be exorcized since they fall into the realm of physical rather than spiritual phenomena. Often, however, those experiencing the memories will be in need of counselling in order to reassure them that the memories do not pose any threat to them. He also believes that the house and its inhabitants should be blessed – in particular the person who, whether consciously or unconsciously, has activated the memory. If the family are Christians, Perry also suggests that the priest should conduct a Eucharist on the premises.

If the place memory is of some particularly sinful activity, it could be reactivated by the present inhabitants of the building deliberately indulging in similar activities. In such cases, says Perry, the inhabitants must either renounce their activities, confess their sins and receive absolution or face the fact that the place memory will continue.

Like place memories, poltergeists are often mistaken for hauntings. Poltergeists are, however, generally held to be produced by some form of psychokinetic energy, usually triggered by someone in the household who is suffering from undue stress. There are, however, those who believe that poltergeists are immature, mischievous but harmless spirits. Allan Kardec, the pseudonym of a nineteenth-century psychic researcher and spiritualist from France, is perhaps the leading figure in this latter camp. Whichever explanation is favoured, most experts agree that it is inappropriate to exorcize poltergeists since, whether their origin is in the unconscious mind or the world of spirits, they are not evil.

Nevertheless, exorcists tend to find that poltergeists are the most common reason for their being called on for help. While some will perform exorcisms, many seek instead to counsel the stressed individual they believe is causing the phenomenon.

The first case Canon Dominic Walker, co-chairman of the Christian Deliverance Study Group, dealt with in his role as exorcist was that of a house infested by a poltergeist.

'The family lived in a lovely council house with quite a large garden,' he recalls. 'They were prepared to move into a tower block to get away from this thing. They were terrified.' He admits, however, that, 'If I hadn't actually seen ornaments and kitchen utensils flying around with my own eyes, I might well have believed the whole family was just psychologically disturbed and imagining things.'

Without that early introduction to the reality of the paranormal, Canon Walker confesses that he still might find it hard to put aside his inbred scepticism of such phenomena.

'Once you have seen these things happen, your whole outlook is forced to go through a radical change,' he says. 'You have to accept that psychological and spiritual influences do have a very real effect and cannot be ignored.'

Before the family contacted Canon Walker, they had been in touch with the local vicar who had sprinkled holy water around their home in an attempt to dispel the poltergeist. Far from improving things, the situation had become much worse.

'Not surprisingly, really,' comments Canon Walker. 'He was using the wrong cure. In this situation, it was as if he was fighting magic with magic whereas what the family needed was counselling.'

In Canon Walker's experience, poltergeists occur when people deny or are cut off from their feelings. This creates tension, a type of psychic energy builds up and activates the poltergeist. With adults, Canon Walker has witnessed poltergeists occurring when the individuals concerned have denied such traumatic experiences as bereavement, infidelity or illness – including cancer and the HIV virus. In one case he witnessed, a poltergeist was caused by a mother who refused to accept that her partner was abusing their child.

Canon Walker estimates that roughly two-thirds of the cases of poltergeist phenomena he has come across have been triggered by adolescents. He has also found that Muslim families often need help with poltergeists.

'The children in Asian families are often required to live

two separate lives – one at home and one at school,' he explains. 'The tension this causes can often give rise to the energy which causes poltergeists.'

More commonly, however, he finds that poltergeists are caused by young people failing to come to terms with the sexual feelings which arise with the onset of puberty.

This was, he discovered, the situation which lay at the root of the poltergeist problem plaguing the family he was first called on to visit. In this particular case, there was a thirteen-year-old boy in the family who was leading a very isolated existence.

'I talked with him alone and as he began to talk, and release the feelings pent up inside of him, the poltergeist died down,' Canon Walker explains. 'It was not the sort of family that talked together and the poltergeist resulted from a lack of communication.'

Michael Perry suggests that, as with 'place memories', the house and its inhabitants might be helped, if they are Christians, by being blessed. The aim, he says, is to calm down the stressed atmosphere and return a feeling of love and unity to the home.

Particularly for those people who have no understanding of them, poltergeists can be extremely disturbing – even terrifying. Generally, they make their presence known by strange rapping and knocking noises. Objects often move to different places around the home or fall over seemingly of their own accord. Lights might switch on and off, doors open and close and sometimes objects will spontaneously break into flame.

One of the most famous historical cases of a poltergeist was that of the so-called Drummer of Tedworth, which occurred in 1661. The drummer of Ledgershall in Wiltshire had been so infuriating the townspeople with his incessant drumming that eventually they had him taken before the legal authorities by John Mompesson who lived in the neighbouring town of Tedworth. The drum was confiscated and Mompesson was asked to take care of it in his own home.

The following month, while Mompesson was away from home, his family was subjected to an outburst of poltergeist activity. A drumming sound was heard outside and above the house and the noise then moved indoors to the room where the drum was kept. The children and servants saw apparitions and some of the children were levitated while in bed. Strange scratching and panting noises were also heard and chairs moved about by themselves. Sometimes the air became hot and smelt foul, sometimes clothes and shoes were thrown about, doors opened and shut seemingly by themselves and an eerie glimmering light was seen. The imprint of claws was found in ashes, and singing was heard coming from the chimney.

One morning, a voice was heard repeatedly saying 'A witch, a witch', which finally convinced the Mompesson family they were suffering from the curse of a demon or even the Devil. A magician offered to perform an exorcism for a hundred pounds but he was turned down.

Eventually the drummer turned up again in a neighbouring town and claimed that he had caused the disturbances as a punishment for Mompesson having taken away his drum. He was charged with witchcraft and many of those who had experienced the poltergeist testified against him. The drummer was eventually banished from the area and the poltergeist activity calmed down. However, wherever the drummer went, he was said to cause storms and whenever he came anywhere near Tedworth, the poltergeist returned.

Those who believe poltergeists are caused by stress would probably claim the Tedworth poltergeist was caused by the Mompesson children: as Canon Walker has already observed, poltergeists often occur in homes where young children are reaching the stage of puberty, a fact he attributes to the phenomena being caused by repressed sexual energies.

On the other hand, those who believe poltergeists are caused by mischievous spirits would say that this was doubtless the case in the Mompesson household. For, even though the poltergeist spirits themselves are not evil, many investigators claim they can be controlled by a malevolent human being.

Three centuries on, in the 1960s, a poltergeist in Pontefract, Yorkshire, was also distinguished by a strange drumming sound and by the presence of children in the afflicted home. The poltergeist was said to have destroyed countless objects around the house and at night made such loud drumming noises that the neighbours would apparently gather outside to listen. In addition, several people claimed to have actually seen the poltergeist which appeared as a monk dressed in black. Apparently, this so-called 'Black Monk' even dragged the teenage daughter of the family upstairs by the throat, although in doing so it caused her no harm.

The house was, it was later discovered, built on the site of a former gallows and a monk had been hanged there for rape several hundred years earlier. In this case, then, it appears that a place memory had become mixed up with poltergeist activity.

The Pontefract poltergeist first made its presence known

in 1966 by creating small pools of water on the kitchen floor – a give-away sign that a poltergeist is on the prowl according to experts. The manifestations soon ceased, but began again two years later. This time, they were far more sensational. The family eventually called in a member of the clergy to exorcize the poltergeist. When he suggested that the strange phenomena were caused by subsidence, a candlestick rose allegedly from a shelf and floated under his nose. The exorcism proved unsuccessful.

The Pontefract poltergeist finally disappeared of its own volition: one day, the children of the household looked on as the Black Monk seemed to melt into the kitchen floor. From that point onwards the family experienced no more supernatural phenomena in their home.

Whereas the Pontefract poltergeist lasted for only a few months, the Tedworth poltergeist was said to be continuously active for more than two years. According to Michael Perry, though poltergeist phenomena can last as long as six months, and in some extremely rare cases for a year or more, it is unusual for them to continue for more than a few weeks.

Exorcists are also regularly called on to exorcize apparitions – figures which appear to exist as real beings but for whom no physical cause can be found. Throughout history, and across all societies, these so-called 'ghosts', whether of the living or the dead, have regularly made their appearance. Some of them may simply be hallucinations, or the result of place memories – in which case the apparition's behaviour will be repetitive to the point of being mechanical. Other ghostly phenomena fall into less well-defined categories.

An apparition of a living person is known as a

'doppelgänger'. One explanation for such a phenomenon is that the person who sees the apparition is thought to receive some sort of telepathic message which takes on the physical characteristics of the person sending the message. Sometimes the person projects himself or herself to another place consciously, sometimes unconsciously.

Frederick Myers, one of the founding fathers of the Society for Psychical Research which was set up in Britain in 1882, conducted a massive study of doppelgängers. He concluded that most made their appearance at times of great crisis, such as illness, sudden danger or death. As a result, such doppelgängers came to be called crisis apparitions.

This explanation of living ghosts seems plausible: telepathy, after countless tests, is beginning to be accepted. The step from there to believing that a telepathic thought projection can take on a visual form is not too great to swallow.

What, however, of apparitions of dead people? Can they, too, create telepathic images of themselves? If so, why do two or more people often see the apparition of a dead person they have no knowledge of at the same time, in the same place, wearing the same clothes and with the same facial expressions? Some people have again explained such phenomena by attributing amazing feats of telepathy to the dead person. They suggest, for instance, that the dead person can telepathically convey an image to a living person who has some knowledge of them and that this living person will in turn convey the image to someone they themselves know, but who has no knowledge of the dead person. Others believe this is simply stretching the limits of telepathy too far. Instead, they insist that ghosts really do exist as real, objective phenomena.

According to Michael Perry who refers to such ghostly apparitions as 'unquiet spirits':

'Occasionally . . . the counsellor is forced to consider as a possible hypothesis that some particular and identifiable individual, though departed this world, is "earthbound", and keeps troubling a person or a place with which during his life he had particularly strong emotional ties.'

Perry leaves it to the individual to decide whether the apparition is a ghost or a subjective hallucination. Whatever the categorization, he once again insists that exorcism is not the cure for such an entity:

'The counsellor will recall that he is dealing with a human soul which needs salvation or guidance, and not with a demonic entity which could be commanded to "depart to its own place".'

Instead of an exorcism, he suggests that a requiem eucharist should be conducted for the departed soul, that prayers should be said for the spirit as well as for those who have encountered it, and that bereavement counselling might also be appropriate for the latter.

Perry's view differs vastly from that held by Christians in medieval England. The Catholic Church taught that ghosts were the souls of those people who were confined to Purgatory and were compelled by God to haunt the land of the living until their sins had been atoned for.

The Reformation put paid to any such notion by claiming that Purgatory did not exist, that the dead went either to heaven or hell and that they were unable to return. Despite this teaching, Protestants still saw apparitions. To account for this, the Reformers taught that ghosts were not the souls of the departed but were almost invariably evil spirits sent to earth by the Devil.

Just as belief in ghosts waned under the early Protestants, so it rose under the Catholics of the Counter-Reformation. In the seventeenth century the Catholic Church produced countless manuals on exorcism giving precise instructions for the exorcism of poltergeists and haunted houses as well as of people possessed by demons.

By the end of the seventeenth century, ghosts began to creep back into the Protestant worldview. The reason was that many people felt that ghosts provided evidence of Christianity – evidence which was much needed as more and more people turned away from Christianity to become confirmed atheists.

Protestants, however, could not turn to exorcists to deliver them from ghosts. During the Reformation, exorcism was viewed as little better than magic and the office of exorcist disappeared from the Ordinal of 1550. According to Bishop John Jewel, one of the fathers of English Protestantism, Christians were no longer to believe that the Devil could be frightened by holy water, the sign of the cross or readings from the Bible. Instead, Protestants had to abandon these tools of the Catholic exorcist and instead turn simply to prayer and fasting in the hope of persuading the evil spirit to depart.

Many people failed to consider mere prayer and fasting a sufficiently strong protection from ghosts and so turned to magicians and wizards for help. One such magician, Robert Tooley of Devonshire, concocted particularly imaginative recipes for ridding his clients of ghostly influences. According to a document dating from the late seventeenth century, he was once confronted with the case of a man who claimed to be troubled by the ghost of a neighbour who had hanged himself.

Tooley told the man's wife to arrange for two men to go, at night, to the grave of the dead man. One man was to stand at the head of the grave and the other at its foot and for an hour they were to flourish their swords in the air while Tooley stood by with a bottle of brandy and wrestled with the spirit. Afterwards, a sword was skewered through the middle of the grave, at which point the man's wife was told she would hear all manner of strange noises in her home.

Meanwhile, the sick man himself was told to strap a newly killed and dismembered owl to his head and the wife was instructed to go to the hanged man's house at midnight and make a pincase from straw that she gathered there. Her husband should wear the pincase under one arm and under the other a horseshoe.

Tooley's advice – which cost twenty shillings – was followed, but the sick man got worse rather than better. (2)

Despite Job's declaration that 'he that goeth down to the grave shall come up no more', many Christians point to the Bible as proof of the reality of ghosts. They cite the tale of the so-called Witch of Endor in I Samuel, Chapter 28.

King Saul, so the story goes, banished all wizards and 'those that had familiar spirits' from the land of Israel. When, however, Israel was threatened by the terrifying strength of the Philistine armies, he was extremely anxious to seek advice from Samuel – but Samuel was already dead.

Saul decided that the seriousness of the situation called for drastic action and so decided to consult the Witch of Endor in the hope that she might be able to make Samuel appear to him. After instructing his servants to hunt down the woman, he visited her in disguise and begged her: 'I

pray thee, divine unto me by the familiar spirit, and bring
me him up, whom I shall name to you.'

At first the woman was afraid, worried that she would
be put to death for disobeying the ban on wizardry and
mediumship. Finally, however, she complied with Saul's
request and raised Samuel from the dead. Samuel asked Saul
why he had gone to the trouble of disturbing him, and on
hearing of Saul's difficulties, told him that he was in distress
because he had disobeyed the Lord.

At the time of the Reformation, Protestants claimed that
the Witch of Endor, far from conjuring up the ghost of
Samuel, instead manifested some form of demon or probably
even the Devil himself.

The New Testament, too, seems to provide a case for
Christians to believe in ghosts. There, Jesus himself talks with
the long dead Moses and Elijah on the Mount of Transfigura-
tion. Not even the early Protestants could deem it suitable
that these two Old Testament prophets should be considered
unclean spirits which needed exorcizing from Jesus.

Today, the more common Christian approach towards
ghosts is to treat them as troubled, earthbound spirits.
Whereas Michael Perry believes they should be laid to rest
with prayer and a special requiem Eucharist, Canon John
Pearce-Higgins believes in using the art of persuasion on
them. Exorcism is to him far too strong a technique to use
on ghosts and instead he will conduct a simple conversation
with the spirit, with the aim of helping it to sort out its
problems and so enable it to leave.

A similar technique is used by Eddy Burke, a psychic
investigator who found he had a gift for dealing with ghosts
and hauntings. He describes his calling as 'the release of
earthbound souls or people'.

Eddy regards exorcists with deep suspicion. He believes that most are so intent on ridding the spirit from the land of the living that they give little thought to its wellbeing or to where they are actually sending it. His approach is to share the spirit's experiences with it. He describes his role as being similar to that of a psychiatrist in that he aims to help the spirit rid itself of emotional blockages which are trapping it in the earthly realm. The intention, he says, is to allow the spirit to relive the situation which has caused it to become trapped.

According to Eddy, some spirits are wary of him at first, particularly if they have already been subjected to an exorcism. Usually, however, he finds that spirits which have been stuck in the earthly realm for a very long time are longing to be released.

'What I do is to go into the haunted building and make contact with whatever entity is there,' he explains. 'If it is an earthbound soul I try and get it to go through the catharsis of the problem that is causing it to be stuck. The problem is usually associated with its death. When we have finally sorted out the problem, other spirits will come to take it away to another level.'

The case of the haunted cattery is typical of the type of situation Eddy is called on to deal with. As he tells the story, he was alerted to the problem by two young women who had recently taken over the cattery, situated in the south of England. Both women had felt there was something not quite right with the atmosphere of the building. Eddy soon solved the problem: it was, he claimed, caused by a tragic accident which had happened to a young groom some years previously.

As a result of chatting to the spirit of the groom, Eddy

discovered that one day the young man, who was in his early twenties at the time, had decided to play a trick on one of his friends. He had thrown a rope over a beam, tied a noose at one end and, standing on a box, put his head through the noose.

'His plan was that when his friend came into the room, he would relax his head on one side and fake a ghoulish expression so that it looked as if he had hanged himself,' Eddy explains. 'His mate, however, didn't turn up for some time and so the groom was left standing on the box with the rope around his neck. The box was balanced on its end and, as time passed, it began to wobble. Eventually, the box fell from under the groom and he was left hanging by his neck. He managed to pull himself up slightly to lift the weight from his neck and he stayed like that for some time. Gradually, though, his strength ebbed away, the rope tightened around his neck and he died the most horrible death.'

According to Eddy, the groom's spirit felt tremendously relieved having shared his memory and was taken away to the world of spirits. The whole process took only twenty minutes to half an hour. The young women at the cattery are now no longer troubled by an uneasy atmosphere: the oppression has lifted and instead the house is filled with a feeling of lightness.

Psychic investigators such as Eddy Burke are a new breed of ghost-buster. In earlier times, priests, magicians or witches used to handle hauntings. Now, while priests still do deal with such cases, the field has opened up to become a form as much of science – some would say quackery – as of religion.

The field of psychic research, or parapsychology – that

is, the study of facts that confound our ordinary explanations for man and his world – began to be developed earlier this century. It arose out of the conflict between science and religion which reached a peak in Victorian times.

In the 1930s, researchers into the paranormal began to make their work more scientific, conducting laboratory experiments in an attempt to discover the truth behind events which seemed to defy normal scientific explanation. Still, though parapsychology wants to be seen as a science – and though ghost-busting for some has become almost a profession – many traditional scientists consider it to be no more than a 'pseudo-science'.

In the latter half of this century, many people have sought to resolve the conflict between science and religion and instead have emphasized the similarities between the two fields. Robin Furman is not one of them. A parapsychologist, he has little time for religion other than to view it as a psychological tool.

'The best friend the Church has ever had is the Devil,' he says. 'It's an excellent psychological ploy. Without the Devil to frighten people, the Church would be out of business.'

There is, of course, some truth in what he says. As we have seen in earlier chapters, people generally find it far easier to believe in evil than in good. The Christian teaching that God is more powerful than this very tangible evil entity, the Devil, has, down the centuries, kept people flocking through church doors. But though Robin Furman pooh-poohs the notion of a Devil, and indeed holds no religious belief, this by no means suggests that he believes it impossible to be possessed. Absolutely not. For as well as being a parapsychologist, Robin Furman styles himself an exorcist.

A small, almost elfish man with a mop of ginger curls now greying, and heavy, thick-rimmed glasses, Robin happily describes himself as eccentric. If he is, it has proved no deterrent to the steady stream of people who seek him out in the hope of being delivered from evil spirits. An examination of the study of Robin's large Grimsby house reveals that this exorcist-cum-parapsychologist certainly has eclectic tastes. A statue of the Buddha nestles next to a crystal on one small shelf, the furniture is heavy, rather forbidding Victoriana and the walls are adorned with the certificate for his degree in psychology from Hull University together with a large picture of the Catholic visionary Padre Pio.

A Catholic visionary gracing the study of an atheist?

'I am not prejudiced against people who have a religious belief,' Robin insists.

What he does object to is the cringing and genuflecting that he sees most religions as encouraging. Moreover, religions are, he believes, simply not very *intelligent*. And it is intelligence that concerns Robin – he litters his conversation with a bewildering number of obscure names and dates. While he considers it rather unintelligent to believe in religions, he says:

'I think there most certainly are external good forces and external evil forces. But not as they're depicted – not in a *simplistic* fashion.'

It is, Robin believes, some form of intelligence, or the mind, which exists after the death of the physical body. According to Robin, this entity might sometimes be called an astral body. He, however, prefers to call it a 'thought form'. A thought form is, he claims, capable of influencing people:

'Once the person has begun to be influenced, they are

weakened. Then, the thought form can begin to take them over, and in the end might take them over completely and so possess them.'

Robin says that people can also create thought forms when they are alive:

'A thought form can possess you and you can get a thought form you have created to possess someone else,' he says. 'Some people might call the thought form a demon. Jung would call it an archetype.'

The thought form, demon or archetype, will, according to Robin, become real in its own right – 'like a computer running away with itself, or Frankenstein's monster'. The person who has created the entity must learn how to control it. It is, he says, through learning how to control thought forms that people are able to cast what are commonly called spells.

'You can exert a mental force in such a way that you can make people feel things at a distance,' he claims. 'There is no doubt,' he adds, 'that you can kill people this way.'

While Robin hasn't gone so far as to kill anyone, he does say, driving his point home with a piercing stare, that he has become 'quite adept' at influencing people through the power of his mind. Such powers are not at the beck and call of just anyone:

'You have to have a brain,' he says – perhaps not surprisingly, given his predilection for the intellectual. 'It is not easy.'

According to Robin, it is possible to experience congenial possession, nasty possession or very pleasant possession. He recalls a pleasant case of possession he himself encountered:

'One of the girls who used to come to my seances would go spontaneously into a trance and quite happily became a cat. She would get up off her chair, get down on the floor and start acting as if she were a huge animal, meowing, purring and occasionally growling and pawing at the carpet with her front feet. Her movements were incredibly supple. Sometimes she would just sit and look at you with a very strange expression. She would keep it up for between half an hour and an hour at a time.'

The woman, a thirty-year-old secretary, would apparently never remember what had happened to her, but would always say she experienced an extreme sense of wellbeing afterwards.

Robin's theory is that the woman may have been possessed by the Ancient Egyptian cat goddess. It is interesting, he points out, that in Ancient Egypt the cat goddess was invoked to get rid of evil spirits. Maybe the cat goddess was protecting the people during the seance.

The Ancient Egyptian cat goddess is not the only possessing entity from times long gone that Robin has encountered. But his brush with Pazuzu, the ancient Mesopotamian demon, was a far from pleasant experience. Coincidentally, Pazuzu crops up in William Peter Blatty's book *The Exorcist*, where he threatens the elderly priest who is eventually called on to exorcize Regan. The suggestion is that it is Pazuzu who has possessed the child.

According to Robin, what he was up against was probably a thought form that had been created thousands of years ago and had come to be dubbed Pazuzu to distinguish it from the other thought forms flying around. He also considers it likely that the longer thought forms exist, the more powerful they become.

As in *The Exorcist*, Robin's alleged encounter with Pazuzu was eventually successful. Unlike the fictional elderly priest, however, Robin did not fight Pazuzu with Christianity. Despite his antipathy towards religion, he is prepared to wield any weapon whatsoever – including Christianity – if it promises to bring him success. He says, however:

'This demon was from a time long before Christianity, and so it was unlikely to respond to Christian threats.'

In Robin's opinion, his most powerful tool in overcoming the thought form-cum-demon was that of his own powers of persuasion.

'I got rid of Pazuzu by talking him away,' he claims. 'I did use threats, but my success really rested on the arguments I used. Being an exorcist is a bit like being a lawyer.'

The case of Pazazu, as Robin tells it, began to unfold when he was phoned out of the blue by a Grimsby businessman. After some gentle prompting, the businessman began to relate the story of his wife Hilary's increasingly bizarre behaviour. To begin with Hilary had been sleeping badly and, on seeking advice from her doctor, had been given some sleeping pills. The pills seemed to solve the problem but she began to suffer from appalling nightmares. In her waking hours, Hilary began to feel as if her life no longer belonged to her – she would be carrying out routine household tasks suddenly to 'come round' and wonder what on earth she was doing.

One night, the man was woken up by his wife who was thrashing around in her sleep, her eyes rolling upwards. Suddenly, her eyes opened wide and she stared around her with a terrifying, almost manic expression. The doctor recommended she take more pills, but Hilary's condition only got worse. Her husband felt let down by the medical establishment which had, he claimed, been unable to offer any useful advice. He had even called in a priest, but Hilary's only response was to hurl abuse at him. Driven to distraction the man had sought out Robin as a last resort.

Robin, together with his wife and son, immediately drove over to the man's home, which was situated in a well-off area on the outskirts of Grimsby. Hilary, whom Robin describes as a pretty woman with a pale complexion and faded auburn hair, was lying motionless on her bed. When Robin spoke to her, she removed her gaze from the ceiling and let it settle on the intruder. There was, claims Robin, no mistaking its force – or its threat – and her face was grossly distorted, like a gargoyle's mask.

Eventually, Robin prompted Hilary to speak.

'I – Am – Not – Hilary,' came the response – each word, according to Robin, sounding like the crack of a whip.

Somewhat taken aback, Robin none the less determined to keep the woman talking. He was rewarded with a stream of obscenities. By now, Hilary was squirming and writhing on the bed and grinding her teeth.

The next time she spoke the woman's voice had a harsh, grating sound. Addressing her husband, the voice informed him that Hilary was no longer his, that the owner of this new voice was now in control of the body. On being questioned, the being eventually claimed to be Pazuzu and said that it would not leave Hilary's body without killing her first.

Robin realized it was time to conduct the exorcism – and quickly. He asked the husband to leave the room.

According to Robin, there are six stages of exorcism: 'First of all comes the sense of a presence, the feeling that something is not quite right with the person in question. The second stage is pretence, when the possessed person will pretend there is nothing wrong with them. Thirdly, there is breakpoint, when the exorcist has to try and persuade the possessed person to communicate with him in some way. Soon afterwards comes the fourth stage when the possessing entity itself will converse with the exorcist. The fifth stage is the clash, or battle, when the exorcist and possessing entity meet each other head on. The sixth and final stage is expulsion.'

Robin was already at the fourth stage – he was conversing with the possessing entity. The demon soon made it clear that it had possessed Hilary in order to gain power. Robin told Pazuzu that this was impossible, since no one believed in demons any more.

The demon immediately challenged Robin, saying, 'You believe in me.'

Robin claimed to believe in the demon simply as a scientific phenomenon, whereupon Hilary began spinning around on the bed and her body began to arch backwards like a hoop.

The fifth stage – the battle – had begun. Robin ordered Pazuzu to leave Hilary. The demon made no reply. Again, he ordered it to go. The demon was clearly losing power: when it replied, it made rather feeble excuses as to why it could not leave the woman. Perhaps, Robin thought, Pazuzu had been drawing on the energy given off by the terrified husband. Now he was gone from the room, Robin reasoned, the demon's energy banks must be running low.

Making the most of his apparent advantage, Robin threatened to burn into the demon with his thought patterns until the monster was destroyed. Having by now gained confidence, he again ordered the demon to depart. Hilary half sat up on the bed, then collapsed. She appeared to have stopped breathing. To Robin's relief, her pulse was still beating. The exorcism had been a success.

Robin remains open-minded as to whether Hilary really had been possessed by an ancient Mesopotamian demon or whether she had simply stumbled across an account of Pazuzu in a book – in *The Exorcist* perhaps – and created a 'living nightmare'.

As far as the exorcist is concerned, Robin believes it is of little importance whether the 'demon' is real or not.

'Exorcism works because if the possessing entity is a true demon and believes in what you say, it will be frightened,' he explains. 'On the other hand, the person you are dealing with may believe themselves to be possessed even if they aren't in the power of a true possessing entity. In cases such as that, if the person has some religious belief or at least some form of residual religious belief, the exorcist can probably persuade them as a form of brainwashing that they have been exorcized, that the demon has been banished.'

While this might indeed be true of disturbances in the realm of the psychological or spiritual, it is certainly not true of organic illnesses. Yet, as we shall see in the following chapter, some people believe that even those diseases which can be cured by a simple course of pills are in fact caused by the Devil and his minions, and can only be truly cured by deliverance or exorcism.

6

Science and Belief

For many Christians today, deliverance forms just a small part of the ministry of healing. To these people, health is not simply a matter of physical and mental fitness but also of spiritual wellbeing.

This holistic approach towards health was the norm in pre-industrial times. The sick were not simply bodies to be patched up and pumped full of pills. Rather, in order for each individual to achieve their full potential as human beings, it was believed that they had to be well in mind, body and spirit.

As a result, the role of healer often fell to religious leaders. And deliverance from demons was often seen to form part of the healing process. In the New Testament there are examples of healing miracles which readily lend themselves to the interpretation that the illness has stemmed from demonic oppression or possession.

In Luke Chapter 13, we hear of 'a woman which had a spirit of infirmity eighteen years, and was bowed together, and could in no wise lift up herself.' Jesus refers to her as a woman 'whom Satan hath bound, lo, these eighteen years . . .'

And in Matthew, Chapter 17, Verses 15–18, a man kneels before Jesus and says: 'Lord, have mercy on my son: for he is lunatick, and sore vexed: for ofttimes he falleth into the fire, and oft into the water. And I brought him to thy disciples, and they could not cure him.' After bewailing this 'faithless and perverse generation', Jesus 'rebuked the devil: and he departed out of him: and the child was cured from that very hour.'

The power of a religion was often judged in accordance with the healing ability of its leaders and healing and deliverance often became tools of evangelism, a way of winning new recruits.

Certainly, this was true of the early Christian Church: the apostles won new converts both through healing miracles and through their ability to cast out evil spirits. According to Acts, Chapter 5, Verses 12–16:

And by the hands of the apostles were many signs and wonders wrought among the people . . . And believers were the more added to the Lord, multitudes both of men and women. Insomuch that they brought forth the sick into the streets, and laid them on beds and couches that at the least the shadow of Peter passing by might overshadow some of them. There came also a multitude out of the cities round about unto Jerusalem, bringing sick folks, and them which were vexed with unclean spirits: and they were healed every one.

Moreover, in Acts, Chapter 8, Verses 5–8 we hear how:

Philip went down to the city of Samaria, and preached Christ unto them. And the people with one accord gave heed unto those things which Philip spake, hearing and seeing the miracles which he did. For unclean spirits, crying with loud voice, came out of many that were possessed with them: and many taken with palsies, and that were lame, were healed.'

By medieval times, miracles had become accepted as the chief way of proving that Christianity was superior to other religions. The *Lives* of the saints were filled with miraculous achievements and particular saints were endowed with the ability to heal specific illnesses. St John and St Valentine were, for instance, believed to excel at curing epilepsy – or 'the falling evil' as it was often known.

Just as it was believed that illness could be cured by supernatural means, so it was believed to be caused by the supernatural. The holistic approach towards healing meant that the dividing line between illness and demonic possession or oppression could become extremely faint. The belief was that the body had been invaded by the illness which consequently needed to be exorcized, or conjured, out.

As a result, healing often became a type of superstitious magic, dependent on charms and amulets rather than on faith. To some extent, the basis for this can be found in the Bible. In Acts Chapter 19 we hear how 'God wrought special miracles by the hands of Paul: So that from his body were brought unto the sick handkerchiefs or aprons, and the diseases departed from them, and the evil spirits went out of them.'

Arnald of Villanova, a fifteenth-century physician, alchemist and an adviser to the Franciscans and popes, gives a sense of where healing stood during his day. In his *Antidotarium*, he describes how a seal should be made from purest gold and to the accompaniment of certain Christian prayers and phrases. In addition, the gold should be melted 'as the sun enters Aries' and engraved 'when the moon is in Cancer or Leo and while the sun is in Aries'.

Thus prepared, the seal will, claims Arnald, work 'against all demons and capital enemies and against witchcraft . . .

No harm can befall the building or occupants of the house where it is. It benefits demoniacs, those suffering from inflammation of the brain, maniacs, quinsy, sore throat, and all diseases of the head and eyes, and those in which rheum descends from the head. And in general I say that it wards off all evils and confers good . . .' (1)

The medieval Church devised countless special healing rituals aimed at expelling evil spirits, often viewed as synonymous with illness, from the body. The most basic of these rituals was the benediction of salt and water.

According to historian Keith Thomas: 'Basic to the whole procedure was the idea of exorcism, the formal conjuring of the Devil out of some material object by the pronunciation of prayers and the invocation of God's name. Holy Water, thus exorcized, could be used to drive away evil spirits and pestilential vapours.' (2)

The methods of a renowned sixteenth-century healer, Margaret Hunt, were typical of her day. After finding out the name of the sick person, she would pray to the Blessed Trinity to heal them from all their enemies. Then she would tell the sick person to say for nine consecutive nights five Paternosters, five Aves and a Creed, followed by three more Paternosters, three Aves and three Creeds. At bedtime they were told to repeat one Paternoster, one Ave and one Creed in worship of St Ives. The woman would administer certain herbs, sometimes mixed with holy water. (3)

Another healer, who specialized in the cure of 'ringworm, tetter-worm and canker-worm', would say three times: 'In the name of God I begin and in the name of God I do end. Thou tetter-worm (or thou canker-worm) begone from hence in the name of the Father, of the Son, and of the

Holy Ghost'. Afterwards, she would apply honey and pepper to the afflicted part. (4)

In everyday practice, then, healing and deliverance went hand in hand. None the less, it is often claimed that the New Testament authors drew a clear distinction between healing miracles and casting out demons. Luke recounts how Jesus sent a message to Herod saying 'Behold, I cast out devils, and I do cures . . .' (5) In the same gospel, Jesus gives his disciples 'power and authority over all devils, and to cure diseases'. (6)

But how were Christians to distinguish between the need for deliverance and the need for straightforward healing? In practice, was it simply that the New Testament writers were so ignorant about medicine that they attributed any illness they failed to understand to demons?

Certainly, down the centuries, the huge misunderstanding surrounding mental illness has caused it to be swathed in superstition and time and again attributed to supernatural powers. It is a belief which the sufferers themselves can often help to bolster: one of the commonest symptoms of delusional insanity is the patient's conviction that he or she is in contact with, or actually is, a supernatural being. So were some of the famous Medieval and Renaissance cases of demonic possession really cases of mental or nervous disorders?

There is, for instance, the example of an exorcism performed by the twelfth-century saint Bernard of Clairvaux who was confronted by a woman who 'ground her teeth and put out her tongue like an elephant's trunk.' Her appearance was, said the saint's biographer, so grotesque that 'she seemed not a woman, but a monster.' Undeterred, St Bernard confronted the demon, saying, 'By the terrible power of His majesty I command thee, evil spirit, to come out of His servant and dare to touch her no more thereafter.' Afterwards, the woman's tongue was restored to its normal size, thereby enabling her to give thanksgivings. (7)

Around the same time, St Norbert of Magdeburg was faced with a particularly stubborn demon which had taken possession of a young woman. Time and again, the demon mocked St Norbert's attempts to send it on its way until at long last, 'strong in the might of the Spirit', the saint was successful. Unfortunately, when the demon abandoned the vessel he had possessed, he left behind 'a trail of unspeakably stinking urine'. (8)

Roughly a century later, a biographer of St Francis of Assisi describes how the saint encountered a man whom some thought to be afflicted by a malignant devil:

> For often-times he was dashed down and with a terrible look in his eyes he wallowed foaming; sometimes his limbs were contracted, sometimes extended, sometimes they were folded and twisted together, and sometimes they became hard and rigid. Sometimes, tense and rigid all over, with his feet touching his head, he would be lifted up in the air to the height of a man's stature and would then suddenly spring back to the earth.

St Francis cured the man by praying, making the sign of the cross over him, and blessing him. 'And suddenly he was made whole, and never afterwards suffered from this distressing infirmity.' (9)

One of the victims of the famous seventeenth-century outbreak of demonic possession at Loudun, which we will look at in more detail later, was, according to a later account, violently shaken backwards and forwards so that her teeth clattered together and strange sounds were forced out of her throat. In addition, 'between these movements her face became completely unrecognizable, her glance furious, her tongue prodigiously large, long and hanging down out of her mouth, livid and dry'. (10)

The account of a case of possession which occurred some hundred years earlier shows more sympathy for the alleged victim. The long-suffering girl was repeatedly attacked by an evil spirit who 'had taken possession of her eyes which he had made start out of her head.' In addition, the demon 'had twisted her tongue and pulled it more than eight inches out of her mouth, and turned her face towards her back with an expression so pitiful that it would have melted a stone.' (11)

Many of these phenomena – including the large tongue, the bent body, the involuntary discharge of urine at the end of the fit – had, as long ago as Ancient Greek times, been regarded as symptoms of epilepsy. This did not, however, take the ailment out of the realm of the spiritual: according to the Ancient Greeks, epilepsy was a sacred disease. As a result, epileptics were often treated with immense respect, amounting at times to awe.

The fact that these alleged cases of demonic possession were cured by exorcism is no proof that the victims were indeed invaded by evil spirits. Autosuggestion is an extremely powerful healing tool.

In 1603, Dr Edward Jorden a writer on witchcraft, observed that the success of charms, amulets and holy water in curing sickness was dependent not on inherent supernatural virtue, but to 'the confident persuasion which melancholic and passionate people may have in them'. One anecdote told by a seventeenth-century Dean of Durham, and repeated by Keith Thomas in his book *Religion and the Decline of Magic*, was that of a French doctor with a patient who was convinced he was possessed by the Devil.

> The doctor called in a priest and a surgeon, meanwhile equipping himself with a bag containing a live bat. The patient was told that it would take a small operation to cure him. The priest offered up prayer, and the surgeon made a slight incision in the man's side. Just as the cut was given, the doctor let the bat fly into the room, crying 'Behold, there the devil is gone!' The man believed it and was cured. (12)

From the seventeenth century onwards, the rise of a mechanistic way of looking at man and the universe put paid to much of the superstition which went hand in hand with the holistic approach towards health. Certainly, many of the illnesses which were long ago attributed to invading spirits are now known to be caused by chemical imbalances. Epilepsy can, for instance, sometimes be attributed to calcium levels in the blood. But can doctors sometimes go too far? The scientific revolution also destroyed much that was good in the realm of healing. Mind became separated from body and healing was seen to belong firmly in the realm of the physical.

With the rise of the profession of psychiatry in the nineteenth century, virtually any religious ecstasy – including voluntary possession such as mediumship – came to be seen as a form of insanity. According to the German theologian, Rudolf Bultmann (1884–1976), who was determined to demythologize the Bible: 'Man's knowledge and mastery of the world have advanced to such an extent through science and technology that it is no longer possible for anyone seriously to hold the New Testament view of the world – in fact, there is hardly anyone who does.' (13)

Exorcism went through a period of decline at this time, but the physician and psychiatrist became a type of secular exorcist. Religious mania was categorized as a specific type of insanity believed to prevail among women and clergymen. Possession, whether voluntary or involuntary, was an illness and it was going to be wiped out, not by exorcism but by the power of science.

Henry Maudsley, the famous nineteenth-century mental pathologist whose name has been given to the Maudsley Hospital in south London, was fiercely opposed to the power of the Church and believed devoutly that science held the key to enlightenment. As far as he was concerned, ecstatic religious experience was linked to epilepsy. He even went so far as to diagnose Mahomet, Saul, Swedenborg and Ann Lee, the founder of the Christian Shaker sect, as epileptics. Religious experiences, along with supernatural powers were, he claimed, abnormal functions of the brain.

Not surprisingly, then, Maudsley firmly believed that mediums, who chose to become possessed in order to commune with departed spirits, were deranged and that spiritualism actually attracted the insane.

Soon, the medical profession as a whole came to believe that there was a direct link between spiritualism and diseased minds. According to an article on mediumship published in the *Lancet* in 1876:

When men and women surrender the privilege, and abrogate the duty, of shaping their beliefs according to the evidence of senses trained and instructed by experience, they place themselves in a position of danger to sanity, which no intelligent being, however confident in his strength of intellect, should risk . . . we think the nuisance and peril of such exhibitions ought to be vigorously and summarily removed.' (14)

A British doctor, Lyttleton Stuart Forbes Winslow, said of spiritualists: 'The community of believers contains a large proportion of weak-minded hysterical women, in whom the seeds of mental disorder though for a time latent, are only waiting for a new excitement to ripen into maturity.'

Hysteria was, at that time, believed to be a disease which only women could suffer from – a belief which had been around since the time of the Greek physician Hippocrates (*c.*460-*c.*377 BC) who claimed hysteria was caused by a disturbance of the womb. According to an American doctor, one of the signs of a hysteric was that they were able to experience visions of spirits whenever they so chose. 'On this principle can be explained many of the instances of spiritualistic hallucinations which have been detailed by inquirers willing to be deceived,' he claimed.

In the 1890s, a French psychologist recorded the manifestations of a hysterical attack:

Suddenly terrible cries and howlings were heard; the body, hitherto agitated by contortions or rigid as if in the grip of tetanus, executed strange movements: the lower extremities crossed and uncrossed, the arms were turned backwards and as if twisted, the wrists bent, some of the fingers extended and some flexed, the body was bent backwards and forwards like a bow or crumpled up and twisted, the head jerked from side to side or thrown far back above a swollen and bulging throat; the face depicted now fright, now anger, and sometimes madness; it was turgescent and purple; the eyes widely open, remained fixed or rolled in their sockets, generally showing only the white of the sclerotic; the lips parted and were drawn in opposite directions showing a protruding and tumefied tongue. (15)

The symptoms bear a striking resemblance to those attributed in medieval times to demonic possession. At the end of the nineteenth century, however, hysteria is the alleged cause.

According to Dr Winslow, spiritualism was 'the curse of our age, and one of the principal causes of insanity in England, and especially of that desponding and melancholic type known as "religious insanity", so prevalent in the present century.' (16)

In time, physicians even came up with a specific name for the mental disorder spiritualists were said to suffer from. These pitiful women were, they said, in the grip of 'mediomania'. The disorder was closely allied to 'utromania', an illness allegedly caused, like hysteria, by a 'wandering womb' and often typified by the woman's desire to embrace spiritualism and sexual immorality. The 'cure' for these women was, on more than one occasion, to be shut away in a mental asylum.

Like the so-called condition of 'mediomania', most reported cases of a condition known as multiple personality disorder date from the second half of the nineteenth century. Again, belief in the condition gained ground as a result of the inerrancy of the Bible having been brought into question: demon possession no longer seemed a plausible explanation for sudden and disturbing changes in personality.

Instead, some physicians claimed that multiple personality disorder was the rational and scientific means of explaining how someone could suddenly manifest 'demonic' characteristics. According to one definition of multiple personality disorder:

> The essential feature is the existence within the individual of two or more distinct personalities, each of which is dominant at a particular time. Each personality is a fully integrated and complex unit with unique memories, behaviour patterns, and social relationships that determine the nature of the individual's acts when that personality is dominant. Transition from one personality to another is sudden and often associated with psychosocial stress . . . Usually the original personality has no knowledge or awareness of the existence of any of the other personalities (subpersonalities). (17)

Both the theory of multiple personality disorder and the theory of demon possession encourage sufferers to see themselves as taken over by alien entities – whether demons or different personalities. Moreover, as with demon possession, there is debate in some circles as to whether multiple personality disorder really exists. Some people say that it is a condition which only appears when it is given credence by society at large and also by the psychiatrist who attempts to treat the disorder. Certainly, with both multiple personality disorder and demon possession, we are in a region where belief systems hold sway over objective reality.

Rather than rolling back the frontiers of enlightened society, belief in multiple personality disorder has, say critics of the theory, merely substituted one myth for another.

Dr Morton Prince of Boston, Massachusetts was one of the key nineteenth-century figures to show an interest in multiple personality disorder. In 1898 he was consulted by Christine Beauchamp, a twenty-three-year-old single woman who was suffering from various nervous disorders. Dr Prince had already published papers on double personality and was known to be fascinated by the condition.

To begin with, Dr Prince attempted to alleviate Christine's condition by means of hypnosis. One day, when under hypnosis, a new personality emerged from the young woman. Sally Beauchamp, as the newcomer called herself, was outgoing and jolly – an almost complete contrast to Christine. Whereas Sally knew all about Christine, Christine knew nothing of Sally. As time passed, Sally began to take over Christine's body for longer and longer periods of time and Christine became increasingly confused. Then a third personality emerged. This one proved to be a rather prim and proper woman. Dr Prince eventually managed to integrate Christine and the prim newcomer. Sally, on the other hand, was not so obliging and had to be 'thrown out' from the body – something which Dr Prince later admitted he had not fully succeeded in accomplishing. Apparently, before leaving Christine's body, Sally created an immense fuss, screaming, 'No, I won't be dead! I have as much right to live as she has . . .' To all appearances, we are back in the land of *The Exorcist*.

Critics of multiple personality disorder have often suggested that Christine was so keen to please Dr Prince that she described her condition in terms that would comply with the alleged symptoms of the disorder. Certainly, Dr Prince, along with other proponents of the multiple personality disorder theory, were later accused of having been duped by mythomaniacs who involuntarily produced the symptoms their physicians wanted to see. Others have accused Dr Prince and his cronies of being straightforward charlatans who colluded with their patients with the deliberate intention of deceiving the medical world.

Certainly, the sensational nature of multiple personality disorder has often brought unprecedented attention to its supporters. For the same reason, the condition has attracted a good deal of attention from the general public. Books such as *The Three Faces of Eve, Sybil* and *The Minds of Billy Milligan* proved best sellers.

The Three Faces of Eve describes how Christine Sizemore manifested two entirely different personalities. One was a meek and obedient married woman, the other was a 'good time gal' who was raucous, flirtatious and fun-loving. It was not, according to Eve's therapists, that she was simply experiencing wild personality swings. Rather, two totally different people inhabited her body at different times: one was Eve White, the other was Eve Black. Eventually, the therapists managed to integrate the two personalities to create a type of Eve Grey. Later, however, Christine Sizemore revealed that her problem returned, in an even more severe form. This time, she claimed to be infested by some thirty different personalities.

Sybil tells the story of a woman who manifested fourteen different personalities. According to medical tests, they all had different brain patterns. Those who believe in multiple personality disorders are anxious to highlight such phenomena. One therapist who claims to have dealt with numerous cases notes:

> Medical conditions have been observed when the body is under the control of one personality that are not present when the body is under control of another. In clients with whom I am familiar, medical conditions such as allergy-induced skin rashes, tumours, cysts, severe headaches and even the signs of pregnancy have been noted when one personality has taken over but have disappeared when other personalities control the body. (18)

It has to be said, however, that this provides no 'proof' that another personality has taken over the body: psychogenic illness is nothing new.

The Minds of Billy Milligan demonstrates the extent to which multiple personality disorder can change a person's behaviour. It also calls into question the extent to which a person suffering from the disorder is responsible for his actions. In 1977 a young man called Billy Milligan was arrested for rape. According to psychiatric tests, Billy was suffering from multiple personality disorder. It was not he who had committed the rape but a lesbian woman. And she was not the only different personality inhabiting Billy's body. Apparently, he consisted of twenty-three different people, one of whom spoke Serbo-Croat, a language of which Billy himself had no knowledge.

Currently, there is a significant rise in the number of patients being diagnosed as having multiple personality disorder. One American therapist recalls listening to a tape about multiple personality disorder in the 1980s. Afterwards, he concluded that two of his patients were suffering from the condition. When he passed the tape on to his colleagues, two of them discovered that they, too, were treating clients who seemed to be multiples. Suddenly, six cases of multiple personality disorder had been uncovered!

What has caused the sudden flurry of cases of multiple personality disorder?

The answer seems to be inextricably bound up with the claim that those suffering from the condition have often been subjected to sexual abuse and, in particular, to Satanic ritual abuse.

One American doctor claims to know of nearly sixty cases of multiple personality disorder in which the patient has, for instance, been subjected to 'forced participation since childhood in Satanistic cult worship entailing ritualistic sex, human sacrifice and cannibalism.' (19)

A murky heap of controversy surrounds the subject of Satanic ritual abuse. Many refuse to believe it actually happens. But to designate a particular psychiatric condition to those who have supposedly suffered from this form of abuse could be seen as an attempt to give it some degree of credence.

Audiocassette tapes about multiple personality disorder have recently been circulating in the United States, and some have found their way to interested parties in other Western countries. One of the tapes outlines a four-factor theory about the development of the disorder.

Factor One is biological – it is generally deemed that about twenty-five per cent of all children are born with the ability to dissociate if they need to. Factor Two has to do with early childhood abuse – about ninety-seven per cent of MPD patients have suffered serious abuse at an early age. Most of them have been abused sexually. They needed to use dissociation to cope with the abuse. Factor Three has to do with continuing abuse and lack of nurture – the life circumstances have been dangerous, and the children continue to suffer abuse over a long period of time. The home is not a safe place, and the child needs to keep on using dissociation to deal with the continuing abuse. Factor Four is about a particular kind of psychological structure some people have – a high ability to fantasize and a high level of creativity.

According to this theory, multiple personality disorder can develop when all four factors are present.

The psychologists, psychiatrists and therapists who believe in the disorder have, it might be thought, destroyed demons in one fell swoop. It would be reasonable to suppose, then, that those Christians who firmly believe in the reality of demon possession would be strongly averse to accepting the theory of multiple personality disorder. Reasonable, maybe, but wrong. Many of those therapists who believe in MPD are, in fact, deeply committed Christians. And some of these therapists discovered that their patients were sometimes possessed both by different personalities *and* by unclean spirits.

Dr Ralph Allison, a leading and highly respected figure within the field of MPD, was the son of a preacher. He discovered that exorcism could prove profoundly helpful to patients and describes the case of one patient, Carrie, who seemed to be suffering from MPD in his book *Minds in Many Pieces*.

A beautiful redhead, Carrie failed to respond to any of

the textbook techniques Allison tried on her. Then a psychic attempted to enter Carrie's mind. Afterwards, he claimed he had come up against an evil presence, that of a dead drug addict called Bonnie, who had taken Carrie over. Eventually, Dr Allison decided to accept that Bonnie was a spirit. His next move was to exorcize her:

> An early session with Carrie had revealed, among other things, that she had once experimented with witchcraft while in high school. She had also once had a boyfriend who was serious about 'black magic'. Her involvement appeared to be typical of the seemingly silly things many high school students do and it did not worry me. However, it did indicate that she believed in the concept of good and evil, of God and the Devil. Thus, I felt that a religious approach such as an exorcism would appeal to her, although I had no intention of talking about Bonnie beforehand. I didn't want to place the idea in her mind, creating a problem where none existed if that proved to be the case.

So it was that Dr Allison came to use the Bible as a type of medical textbook from which he learnt how to cure his patient:

> It seemed fairly simple as I interpreted it. An exorcist must call out each demon by name, then command it to leave in the name of the Holy Trinity – Christ, God the Father, and the Holy Spirit.

Dr Allison also wanted to fit Carrie's preconceptions of an exorcist, and so during the 'treatment', he spoke in a booming voice and commanded the evil spirit to enter a crystal ball he dangled in front of the girl.

In the name of God, the Son, and the Holy Ghost, Bonnie – leave Carrie, leave Carrie in peace! I command you, Bonnie, leave Carrie! By all that's holy, go! Wherever spirits go, go there and leave Carrie! When the crystal ball stops swinging, then Bonnie will be gone and Carrie will be at peace.

To Dr Allison's astonishment, the crystal ball began to swing round and round in a circle. He told Carrie to raise her finger when Bonnie left her. As the ball began to slow down, so Carrie lifted up the designated finger.

After the exorcism, Carrie admitted that she had always felt 'there was something, a spirit or a vision or a shadow of something' with her, but that the feeling had now disappeared, and with it the haunting evil feeling that she was going to die. Carrie was, however, still possessed by other personalities. She eventually committed suicide.

Dr Allison describes five levels of spirit possession which he claims to have encountered. First comes compulsive neurosis such as alcoholism, then multiple personality, then possession by the mind of another human being and then possession by discarnate human spirit. The fifth type of possession Dr Allison describes is that undertaken by non-human spirits.

More recently, American therapist James Friesen recalls working with his first case of MPD, a patient called Beth. A month into treatment, he claims to have been 'pretty certain' he was working with at least fourteen different alter personalities. Nine months later, however, he discovered that he had been wrong: 'Negative Voice', one of the supposed alter personalities, turned out to be none other than an evil spirit.

Friesen describes how at one stage during his work with Beth they seemed to come up against a brick wall: the young woman was clearly troubled by something but despite trying numerous therapeutic tactics, Friesen was unable to help her. Then, during one session, he noticed that she appeared to be suffering from a pain in her neck. Something clicked. He remembered how other therapists had told him that they had found spirits lodged in their patients' necks and shoulders. The patients' physical and emotional problems had cleared up when the spirits were expelled.

Friesen clearly recalls his next line of action: 'Without asking her if I had her permission to make any spiritual intervention, I just said calmly, "In the name of Jesus I command you to come out of Beth and never return." '

All of a sudden, Beth felt better. The soreness in her neck vanished, and her mind was suddenly clear. 'We were both so astonished that we hardly knew what to say!' says Friesen. Looking back on what had happened, however, he and Beth reasoned that 'Some kind of spiritual foe had been uncovered in her therapy, and it tried to disguise itself as a personality. It had spread fear and confusion, so it would not be recognized as a spirit.' (20)

Friesen insists that he neither looks for, nor expects to find demons inhabiting his clients. None the less, he is adamant that time and again they make their appearance. Experience has taught him to recognize when he is dealing with evil spirits rather than alter personalities:

When demons 'manifest' it is different from the way an alter 'takes executive control of the body . . .' A different quality, a different image seems to emanate from demons as opposed to alters. Demons are vile. They work against the personality system. They remain external; they promote fear and confusion, and they do not form relationships with people . . . Demons flit in, strike or accuse, and instantly vanish. They are a nuisance and a pestilence, and the fear they spread can paralyse the whole personality system. When a raspy, low male voice takes over a petite woman's body, and foam begins to form around the edges of her mouth, and the voice says things like, 'She's mine! I will not let her go!' – that is not a personality. The client's vision of the dastardly entity who has spoken confirms its demonic nature . . . To treat such a thing as part of the personality system is to invite chaos for the future. (21)

For Graham Baldwin, a pastor with the Assemblies of God, now based at their training college in the north of England, the distinction between alter personalities and demons is not so clear-cut. Graham's first encounter with the deliverance ministry came when, in his counselling work with London students, he began to be faced with young people who were convinced they were possessed. To gather some idea of Graham's approach to exorcism, it is worth taking a brief look at some of the cases of alleged possession he has come across.

A typical example was that of a young man who asked Graham to deliver him from the demon of lust. Previously, he had sought help from a church whose members had attempted to deliver him. Despite their efforts, his feelings of lust continued unabated. Graham's solution was simply to tell the young man his feelings were perfectly natural, and that he should be grateful for them. If, however, he wanted to control his feelings, he should, Graham suggested, stop spending so much time alone with his girlfriend in her college room. On hearing this advice, the young man was quite upset.

'He was trying to excuse his behaviour by saying it was something outside himself, that it was a demon driving him to want to carry on with his girlfriend,' Graham explains.

It is a tendency which Graham frequently encounters: people will, he finds, deliberately fool themselves that they are possessed in order to evade responsibility for their actions. On other occasions, however, he feels that the individual may be suffering from multiple personality disorder. He views MPD as a type of unconscious coping mechanism.

'A child who has been abused will often have one "demonic" character,' he explains. 'It will be this demonic character which will have undergone the abuse and will have told the child what to do. For the child to view himself as having gone through this ordeal is simply too horrific for them to contemplate.'

Another case Graham encountered was that of a woman who for years had repeatedly thrown fits, especially when she was in a Christian setting such as a church. During services, the woman would start rolling on the floor and speaking in a strange voice. Several members of the congregation thought she was demonized.

As far as Graham was concerned, the woman's behaviour smacked of someone suffering from multiple personality disorder. He suggested to the pastor dealing with the situation that perhaps the woman had been sexually abused when she was a child. The supposition proved to be true. The pastor then concluded that the woman had unconsciously created a demonic character in order to deal with the horrors of her past. Deliverance would, he believed, be totally inappropriate and, more than that, would only worsen her condition. If the woman were delivered and her fits continued – as they might well do since they were apparently not caused by demonization – then she could come to view herself as a lost cause, fit only for damnation. The woman would, the pastor decided, be best helped by counselling.

On another occasion, Graham was confronted with a young woman who claimed she had been offered to Satan as a child and insisted that, as a result, she was possessed by demons. She also claimed that she had been ritually abused during Satanist ceremonies. It took Graham about six months to extract the full story of the girl's past from her. Sometimes, during counselling sessions, the girl would swing into a new voice to describe her experiences. Graham believes that the strange voice indicated that an evil personality had temporarily taken the girl over. He admits that his natural inclination was to believe that the girl was possessed:

'I thought, "This fits in with my theology." Then I heard about multiple personality disorder.'

The problem then arose as to whether the girl was possessed by a demon or simply by a demonic personality. According to Graham:

'The fact that someone who has been severely sexually abused might unconsciously manifest a demonic personality as a coping mechanism by no means indicates that the person is demon possessed. It does not, however, rule possession out.'

Graham began to read some of the accounts of MPD which had been published in the United States. He recalls how one book advised the counsellor not to be worried about the appearance of demonic personalities and that the best course of action was to attempt to be friends with each one of them. So, when the girl started snarling and speaking in a strange voice, Graham began to talk to the 'demon'.

'I told it that it was very good at its job, and continued to talk to it very rationally,' he says.

From time to time, other personalities would also take the girl over. Graham recalls how he was driving with her in his car one day when she suddenly switched personalities to become a young teenager.

'This sixteen-year-old was totally confused,' he recalls. 'She didn't know who I was, or why she was in the car with me. She was terrified and tried to get out.'

Many psychiatrists and psychologists would simply conclude that the girl had regressed. According to Graham, however:

'If she had switched into a younger personality in the middle of a counselling session, I might well have thought she had simply regressed. But to switch suddenly, in the middle of everyday life, is most unusual.'

Another factor which did much to convince Graham that the girl was suffering from MPD was the way in which she would go through total personality changes. One personality, for instance, was aggressive whereas another was promiscuous.

As time wore on, the girl, who had also been having psychiatric care, seemed to improve, but only by the merest fraction. It began to seem unlikely that she would make a full recovery.

Then, one night, the situation reached a crisis point.

According to the girl's account, a being crawled into her bedroom through the window and ordered her to kill herself. The girl was staying with Graham and his wife, Barbara, at the time. Graham was downstairs and Barbara was in the room next to the girl. At the same time, both of them sensed a strong presence of evil.

'It was an awareness that something wasn't right – a sense of dread, of something horrible happening,' Barbara recalls.

Graham hurried upstairs, flung open the girl's bedroom door and was confronted with the sight of the girl half hanging out of the wide-open window. Calmly, he pulled the girl back in, closed the window and then he and his wife prayed together for the girl.

'I said that the evil being had no right to be in our house and commanded it to go,' he recalls.

There was no fuss, no histrionics, this 'being' simply disappeared. Afterwards, the girl was more relaxed than she had been in weeks and felt much better. When, however, Graham told the girl's psychiatrist what had occurred, the psychiatrist said Graham had simply made the girl feel better through the power of autosuggestion rather than having actually delivered her.

None the less, Graham is now convinced that at least a small part of the girl's problem was due to her being possessed and that it was that part which was by far the easiest to deal with.

The Assemblies of God, of which Graham is a pastor, is a Pentecostal denomination. Healing was at the heart of the Pentecostal movement from its outset and the early twentieth-century revival of Pentecostalism played a large part in the upsurge of the ministry of healing.

The healing revival was fuelled in part by a reaction against the overmechanistic approach to health which was evident in the late nineteenth century. But the zeal and fervour of many of those who believe in the ministry of healing can sometimes get out of hand.

While the holistic approach towards healing clearly has a lot to be said for it, it also opens the door to superstition – and to guilt on the part of the sick person. How helpful is it for that person to believe that they have been invaded by evil spirits?

Some hard-line Christians believe that they should leave their health in God's hands – even to the extent that they will throw away their pills, or recommend others to do so. For Christians such as these, illness often comes to be viewed as an outward sign of sin. After all, they say, when Jesus cured the man of palsy in St Matthew's gospel, he said, 'Go away, your sins are forgiven you.'

According to the American preacher Jerry Savelle: 'Not only is it God's will to heal, it is God's will to heal all! Satan is the author of sickness and disease.' (22)

Another American evangelist, Kenneth Copeland, teaches that 'Divine health is the ultimate privilege of every born-again, Spirit-filled believer' and that 'God intends for every believer to live completely free from sickness and disease.'

Copeland has 'World Offices' in Canada, Australia, England and South Africa as well as the United States. One of the many booklets circulated by his Ministries contains his 'Prayer for Health and Healing':

Satan, I speak to you in Jesus's name and I proclaim that your principalities, powers, rulers of the darkness of the world, and spiritual wickedness in heavenly places are

bound from operating against me in any way. I am loosed
from your assignment. I am the property of Almighty
God and I give you no place in me . . . Now, Father,
I believe Your Word that says, 'The angel of the Lord
encamps round about me and delivers me from every
evil work. No evil shall befall me, no plague or calamity
shall come near my dwelling . . .' (23)

For followers of such preachers, ill health becomes a sign
of possession by evil spirits. One Christian fellowship in the
United States was eventually disbanded when its 'curative'
practices came to light: a young boy dying of untreated
diabetes was reportedly spanked 'to try to make him confess
sin they believed was causing the illness'. (24)

According to the late Pentecostal minister, Hobart
Freeman, medicine was a derivative of pagan religion and
as such, evil. Freeman's followers were not even allowed
to wear spectacles. By 1984, it was reported, more than
ninety unnecessary deaths had occurred among his followers
as a result of their having refused medical attention.

Christians do not, however, have to be followers of such
extreme religious leaders to pick up the message that illness
is synonymous with sin. Such thinking can permeate many
Christian groups where a belief in the inerrancy of the Bible
and the miraculous power of Jesus in the world today hold
sway.

Jane, a bubbly woman in her late thirties, knows what
it's like to be on the receiving end of such thinking. For
her, illness became confused with sin and a sign of her failings
as a Christian.

When she was just twenty-one, Jane had a straightforward
appendicitis operation but afterwards developed an infection

which went from bad to worse. It became very severe peritonitis and led to an abscess bursting internally.

'I have been close to dying on several occasions and have had many, many major operations,' she says.

Now, she has to have operations to mop up the effects of the first operations and often suffers a lot of pain.

Jane was already a Christian when she had her first operation.

'Other Christians kept telling me that God would make me better soon if he loved me,' she says. 'Because I wanted God to love me, it put me off being honest with the hospital about how much pain I was in,' she says. 'That really led to my abscess bursting.'

Back in hospital for another operation, Jane again found herself surrounded by Christians.

'When it seemed that I was dying, some of the Christians came and said they would raise me from the dead, that it was going to be a wonderful miracle. I was feeling so ill, so terrible, that was the last thing I wanted. Being left in a lot of pain is no fun.'

Eventually, Jane began to feel that she was in a wilderness of pain – that God had deserted her along with her health.

'I felt I couldn't be praying in the right way, or that I hadn't done the right things in my life,' she says.

Jane is still a Christian. Her experience with pain has, she says, increased her faith. But she treats with caution all those who believe God will provide instant cures.

'Sometimes it happens, and that is lovely for them. But other people watching seem to think it is their right to have the same thing.'

Another woman who suffers from severe arthritis recalls how, when her church was taken over by a charismatic vicar, she came under immense pressure from members of the newly inspired congregation to prove her sin-free state by throwing away her pills.

Many Christians clearly suffer from the belief that their illness is the work of Satan – or proof of their own lack of faith. They long to be delivered from their illness, not only in order to be relieved of suffering but also as proof both to themselves and the world at large that they are indeed committed Christians, worthy of God's love. And yet, despite the anguish which the lack of a healing miracle can cause, there is considerable doubt as to whether, in this day and age, healing miracles actually occur.

Dr Peter May, a GP from Southampton and a member of the General Synod, has yet to be convinced that healing miracles happen today. He has been looking for evidence of one for nearly twenty years. Every case he has investigated has, he says, 'either evaporated before my eyes or changed its character substantially.' Dr May is especially wary of the huge publicity surrounding supposed miracle cures – the books, the videos and the countless public appearances made by people who have allegedly experienced instant recovery from incurable illnesses.

One video currently going the rounds claims that a woman confined to her wheelchair for twenty-five years was 'healed' instantly at a meeting, rose from her wheelchair and ran around the auditorium. After examining the case, Dr May concluded that, though she made use of a wheelchair for more than a year, 'It does not appear that she was at any stage *confined* to a wheelchair.'

'It is a very sad state of affairs,' he says. 'These books and these stories just raise people's expectations and leave them

feeling guilty if they remain ill. It has got to the stage where
if any young person develops a terminal disease, someone
will come along and say if you trust in God you will be
cured. It might offer some people hope, but it condemns
a lot more people to intense emotional suffering.'

As far as the Reverend David Howell, director of the
London-based Church's Council for Health and Healing,
is concerned, healing miracles do indeed occur today. He
claims to have known people who have been 'most
wonderfully and completely healed of cancer, when their
condition has been medically confirmed.' None the less,
he is extremely anxious to avoid the tendency he sees in
some Christian circles to overemphasize the need for
deliverance within the healing ministry. 'Deliverance has
a place within the healing ministry, but no more than that,'
he says. 'It is extremely important not to get it out of
proportion.'

The Council was founded in 1944 by Archbishop William
Temple in an attempt to rediscover the holistic approach
towards healing. His aim was to recover the concept of a
person's spiritual wellbeing being vital to their health. He
believed that modern clinical medicine had become a type
of 'spare-part surgery'. Instead, rather than viewing the body
as a system of mechanical parts, he wanted to return to a
form of healing which saw people as consisting of a soul
and spirit, as well as flesh, bones and blood.

According to the Reverend Howell: 'Where you have
to be extremely careful is not to confuse someone who is
mentally ill with someone who is in need of deliverance
from a power of evil. The distinction is very elusive but
an awful lot of harm can be done if the diagnosis isn't right.'

The difficulty of making this distinction is highlighted in an article on psychiatry and the occult which appeared in *The Practitioner* in 1981 and is cited in Michael Perry's book *Deliverance*. Its authors, David Gill and J. Guy Edwards, point out how organic and psychological symptoms of illness can exist side by side. They illustrate their point with the example of a seventeen-year-old girl who had true epilepsy, hysterical epileptiform fits and consciously feigned attacks:

Her bizarre behaviour at school was alien to her gentle disposition. Because her 'epileptic attacks' were not successfully treated, the rumour that she was possessed by a demon spread within the school. Children and teachers described how they had a strange feeling in her presence, as if someone inside was looking through her eyes and laughing at them. Psychiatric explorations revealed that her strict parents never allowed her to ventilate her feelings through normal channels and that a grief reaction after the death of her grandmother was unresolved. Her abnormal behaviour disappeared after treatment along psychotherapeutic lines.

According to Anglican priest the Reverend Andy Arbuthnot 'A tremendous number of psychiatric disorders are caused by spiritual problems.' He believes there are 'hundreds of thousands of people in psychiatric hospitals who could be freed from their suffering by the deliverance ministry.'

Mr Arbuthnot leads the London Healing Mission, a Christian healing centre which opened its doors in 1948, four years after the Church's Council for Health and Healing was founded.

Since its foundation, the London Healing Mission has

been based in a large Georgian house in west London. Visitors are ushered in by hushed-voiced staff and shown upstairs to a half-landing. There, the fusty atmosphere smacks of an old-fashioned doctor's waiting room but for the fact that the reading material on offer consists of healing testimonies and Christian paperbacks rather than outdated copies of *Country Life*.

The heavy sense of peace is eventually broken by the steady, rhythmic sound of a woman's voice issuing from behind a closed door on the top landing: 'Out under the power of the cross of Jesus and the blood of Jesus . . . Get out under the cross of Jesus and the blood of Jesus . . . Get out . . . Get out . . . Out in the name of Jesus. Out in the name of Jesus. Get out. Get out . . . Out under the power and love of Jesus . . . Out under the power and love of Jesus . . . Out . . . Out . . . OUT.'

Then, all is quiet once more. A door slams and a tall, grey-haired man in a striped shirt, sleeves rolled up, appears. The Reverend Arbuthnot's bearing still betrays his former career as a merchant banker, a profession he left in late middle-age to pursue the Christian ministry full-time. He apologizes for the delay – the young man he and his wife Audrey are busy delivering has proved a tougher nut to crack than they first thought. He disappears again but within half an hour, their mission is accomplished.

Inside the deliverance room, a crucifix lies on the floor, another hangs on the wall and a goblet of red Dubonnet stands, half empty, on a desk. 'John' sits on a settee, his head bowed down and face averted. Tattoos cover his arms and neck, his hair is shaggy and he twitches and jerks as he speaks. Earlier that day, John had taken the train up from the south coast, convinced that his one line of hope lay in Andy and

Audrey's ministry; he was confident that, with their help, the evil spirits he could feel battling for his soul would be put to flight once and for all.

John had come across Andy and Audrey's work just a few weeks previously, while staying in a Christian rehabilitation centre for drug and alcohol abusers. While there, he had listened to Audrey speak on a cassette tape about the healing power of Jesus and about their work at the London Healing Mission. Having abused drugs for the past ten years, starting on LSD at the age of fourteen, John had become convinced that his habit had opened wide the gates for evil spirits to enter his body.

'I felt I needed deliverance,' he mumbles, head still averted. 'I felt I had asked devils into my life.'

Three hours after his session with Andy and Audrey had begun, John looked strained and exhausted, on the point of tears. Audrey took him downstairs for a cup of tea while Andy recounted the afternoon's events.

According to Andy, John was an unusual case in that he had come to them already convinced that his troubles stemmed from his having fallen away from God.

'He wanted to re-give his life to the Lord and so we prayed down the Holy Spirit on him,' he explains. 'For about an hour, the Holy Spirit was very powerfully on him – you could actually see a type of radiance.'

Then, however, the demons began to manifest themselves. Andy described how the young man began screwing up his face in pain, then relaxing, then once again manically contorting his features.

While the Holy Spirit was on him, John had, says Andy, been given the gift of discernment. So, as the demons left the young man one by one, his newly acquired gift enabled

him to name them. Among the evil entities which made
their exit were the spirit of death, the spirit of fornication,
the spirit of Jezebel, Lucifer and the Queen of Heaven (not
to be confused with the Virgin Mary, Andy hastens to point
out).

Andy and Audrey are not the least bit surprised by John's
behaviour. Since taking over the London Healing Mission
in 1983, they have been struck by the huge rise in demand
for deliverance. These days, they say, nine out of ten people
they deal with are troubled by evil spirits. They often find
that not just one, but a whole hierarchy of evil spirits must
be expelled from a person. On one occasion, Andy found
he was casting out unclean spirits at the rate of one every
twenty-five seconds. Bored by the procedure, he began to
cast them out in bundles.

'I always know when an unclean spirit has come out
because the person will cough or sneeze,' he explains.

While insisting that their ministry is focused on healing
rather than deliverance, Andy and Audrey believe that the
two fields are inextricably bound up with one another. In
part, they support their belief with the now well-accepted
medical claim that many illnesses are stress-related. Demons
are, they say, inevitably going to cause stress as they fight
for control over the individual they have invaded. Andy
and Audrey's aim is to bring people to a totally stress-free
way of life, to the 'peace which passeth all understanding'.
Time and again they find that in order to fulfil their mission
they are called upon to cast out demons.

According to Andy, there is a sense in which all illness
originates from sin.

'If God is good and perfect – and I believe Him to be
so – He must have created the world perfect in the first

place,' he says. 'Sickness ultimately comes from Satan. In turning his back on God, mankind allowed Satan and sickness into the world. It was when mankind rebelled against God that things started to go wrong with people's health.'

Andy believes that we all suffer from other people's sins and that consequently, one person's sin can cause illness in another. He illustrates his belief with the example of his niece who was living in a Christian community:

'One particular day, she was fed up with her house mother,' he recalls. 'All day long, my niece was criticizing her in her mind. At the end of the day, the house mother came up to her and said "I have an awful migraine, will you pray for me?" My niece immediately owned up that she had been thinking bad thoughts about the house mother and apologized. The headache went away instantly.'

While believing that sickness ultimately comes from Satan, Andy and Audrey are quick to point out that not all illness is caused by evil spirits. Andy recalls how a distraught young woman turned up on his doorstep one day.

'It turned out that though she had been coming to us for healing, she had gone to someone else for deliverance. Although this person had battled away, they couldn't get anything out of her. The woman naturally became convinced that she was possessed by an extremely stubborn demon. She was so distressed that she actually took an overdose. I told her that the simple reason why they couldn't rid her of the demon was that there was nothing inside her to be cast out. When she finally left us, she was at peace.'

Andy and Audrey's own daughter was similarly frightened: 'A friend of ours purported to cast out the demon of rheumatism from my daughter. A week later she phoned

me up and said, "Dad, I'm still suffering. Does that mean
I've got a demon crawling round inside me?" ' Andy soon
set her mind at rest.

None the less, Andy and Audrey are in no doubt that
some diseases are caused by unclean spirits. Interestingly,
Audrey cites those diseases which are as yet not fully
understood by the medical world, among them cancer and
ME. This attitude immediately begs comparison with New
Testament times when, according to many liberal Christians,
it was lack of medical knowledge which led people to
attribute illness to evil spirits.

Andy and Audrey admit that they occasionally have
difficulty in distinguishing whether a sick person is in need
of deliverance or healing. Sometimes, they find that when
a person is troubled by unclean spirits, the spirits will manifest
themselves in a variety of easily recognizable ways. The
demons might compel the person to roll on the floor, pull
grotesque faces or contort their hands so that they look like
claws.

'Often, you will find that people will writhe along the
floor like a snake,' says Audrey. 'Or the unclean spirit
will speak in a different voice from the person. Sometimes, a woman will speak with the voice of a man, or
a man with the voice of a woman. Occasionally, the demon
will bark like a dog or meow like a cat.' While admitting
that this can seem bizarre in the extreme, Audrey says,
'We've been doing this for ten years and now nothing
surprises us.'

At other times, however, the evil spirits lie low in an
attempt to fool whoever is attempting to deliver them into
thinking they are not there. Then, Audrey and Andy will
use the gift of discernment to establish whether or not the

person is demonized. Sometimes, they will test the person by 'confronting them with the power of Jesus'.

Experience has taught Andy and Audrey that consecrated wine has an inherent spiritual power.

'Often, when we have given a chalice to a person who is demonized, there is an outburst of rage,' says Andy. 'The unclean spirit simply can't handle the power they are confronted with.'

Audrey recalls how she had been talking to someone who was clearly in the grip of unclean spirits:

'When the next person came to see me, they opened the door and simply collapsed on the floor saying there was a satanic presence in the room,' she says.

By sprinkling consecrated wine around the room, the presence was dispelled. Andy and Audrey have also found that if they bless ordinary kitchen tap water and offer it to someone who is demonized, the person will scream out in pain: to them, it seems scalding hot.

The couple also claim that crosses have spiritual power – some more than others. Picking up a wooden cross that had fallen to the floor under Audrey's chair, Andy observes:

'This cross has far more power than the one hanging on the wall. Ten years ago I would have thought anyone who believed in such things was simply in the grip of some ridiculous superstition, but experience has shown me that it is true.'

Much of Andy and Audrey's ministry is focused on inner healing, which Andy describes as 'anything which releases the person to be more totally themselves'. He adds that, while the person is set free in a different way from deliverance, 'inner healing and deliverance often go together.' To illustrate his point, he cites the case of a respectable churchgoing woman who came to him for inner healing:

'She told me that her father had abused her sexually and would give her pocket money if she had sexual intercourse with him. I asked her whether she had confessed to the sin of prostitution. She was horrified, but eventually admitted I was right. Whereas in the past, people had told her that she shouldn't worry and she mustn't feel guilty, I told her that she should repent before Jesus. Afterwards, I ministered absolution to her and suddenly she shouted out and said a pain which had been troubling her for years had completely disappeared.' That, according to Andy, is inner healing and its reflection in physical healing.

Andy admits that he has used his experience of healing miracles as a tool of evangelism. In a religion which he sees as weakened by liberalism, he believes the Christian ministry of healing gives concrete evidence of the power and reality of Jesus.

As can be seen, however, the revival of the Christian healing ministry has also unleashed a host of demons. Some Christians, keen to revive what they regard as a Golden Age of holistic healing, seem to have forgotten that this was also an age of rampant superstition. Many of those individuals who seek healing and instead find themselves being exorcized must wonder whether the price is worth paying.

Liberation or Tyranny?

The claim to be possessed by some spiritual being, whether good or evil, has repeatedly been used as a means towards gaining earthly ends. The sinner who says, 'I was possessed by Satan', can deny responsibility for their actions and expect sympathy rather than punishment. On the other hand, someone can attempt to justify and sanction their actions by claiming to have received a message from God. And who can argue with them? The claim to be possessed by some supernatural power defies logical or rational argument and so is a particularly effective weapon. It is one which has been used throughout history.

The influence of the Delphic oracle is believed to have been enormous. According to one historian. 'All that European Hellas became from the ninth century (BC) onwards . . . was essentially the outcome of the influence of Delphi . . .' (1) Oracles were the method by which, long before the time of Christ, the ancient gods were believed to communicate with the world of mortals. Those who transmitted the gods' messages were believed to become possessed by the deity.

The Delphic oracle was the most important oracle in Greece. It provided individuals and states with advice about religion, personal problems, business and colonial projects and was presided over by Apollo, the symbol of light and nurturer of civilization. He set up base there after killing the Python, a snake deity that lived near by. The name of

Python, or Pythia, was given to the women who delivered the oracles. Little is known about how the women were chosen, although the Greek historian Plutarch (*c.*AD 46–*c.*120) records how the Pythia of his day was the daughter of a poor farmer, a woman of honest upbringing and respectable life, but with little education or experience of the world.

Although there is very little precise information about how the oracles were conducted, it is generally believed that, before pronouncing an oracle, the Pythia would perform a ceremonial bathing ceremony and then, wearing a golden headdress and long robes, drink from a special spring, chew the leaves of a laurel, Apollo's sacred tree, or hold a laurel branch. (Professor T. K. Oesterreich (1880–1949), an expert on the subject of possession and from whom much of this information comes, himself tried chewing laurel leaves in an attempt to discover whether they had any effect. He recorded none of any interest. Similarly, C. W. Goettling, a nineteenth-century academic, drank from the five so-called 'poetic springs' of Greece in the hope of finding himself suddenly inspired. Again, much to his disappointment, he registered no effect whatsoever.)

Having prepared herself, the Pythia would then take her seat on a specially constructed tripod platform, Apollo's ritual seat. According to some accounts, the tripod was placed above a cleft in a rock from which special vapours arose – vapours which many believed to be the cause of the Pythia's state of ecstasy. Both the chasm and the vapour theory have, however, since been disproved by excavations at the site of the oracle. While in the state of enthusiasm, frenzy, or ecstasy, the Pythia would be filled by the presence of Apollo who would speak through her. Usually, the oracles would be interpreted by priests before being passed on to the waiting enquirer. Apparently, the Pythia always died young as a result of the extreme excitement they experienced.

As far back as ancient Greek times, then, possession seems to have been a condition that women rather than men were particularly prone to – or a gift with which they were said to be endowed. It was, however, a power which men felt uneasy about.

Long before Apollo took over the oracle at Delphi, it was ruled over by a female deity – the earth goddess Gaia. Even in those days, the oracles were pronounced by a woman known as the Pythia, but they were interpreted by priestesses rather than priests. The shrine was protected by a snake – and snakes had long been associated with the power and energy of women. Then along came the male god Apollo who killed the snake, thus destroying the symbol of female energy, and took over the shrine. In the centuries that followed, the special powers of the female Pythia were controlled and conscripted by men.

This Delphic oracle formula, whereby a woman's special powers are controlled by men, is paralleled today in Ghana, West Africa. There, the Ga priests are accompanied by female followers who act as mediums for messages from the gods. At religious rituals, the women become possessed by a particular god and pass his utterances on to the priests. Before becoming mediums, the women have to go through up to three years' training.

Even the early Christians did not deny the power of the Delphic Oracle. They claimed, however, that the messages the Pythia relayed via the priests came not from a god but from a demon. The fact that the prophecies proved true was, claimed these Christians, due to the demons having originally been servants of God as a result of which they knew of God's divine plan for mankind.

Both the early Church Father Origen (185-254) and Chrysostom (*c.*347-407), an early Archbishop of Constantinople, believed in the oracles, but they held the view that Apollo was an evil spirit. What the men seem to have found most offensive was the manner in which, so they claimed, Apollo entered the Pythia. In their opinion, the god found his way into the woman through her sexual organs. This accusation has its parallel in later times, when female witches were said to have sexual intercourse with the Devil on a regular basis. Like most religious ecstasy, possession is riddled with sexual overtones. In almost all cases from ancient times, those who become 'possessed' are women and the possessing entity is male. The divine being 'enters' the woman who becomes 'filled' by the god – or devil. According to Origen:

It is said of the Pythian priestess, whose oracle seems to have been the most celebrated, that when she sat down at the mouth of the Castalian cave, the prophetic spirit of Apollo entered her private parts; and when she was filled with it, she gave utterance to responses which are regarded as divine truths. Judge by this whether the spirit does not show its profane and impure nature, by choosing to enter the soul of the prophetess not through the more becoming medium of the bodily pores which are both open and invisible, but by means of what no modest man would ever see or speak of. And this occurs not once or twice, which would be more permissible, but as often as she was believed to receive inspiration from Apollo.

It was clearly all too much for a man who was so determined to retain his sexual purity that he castrated himself. Then, as now, exorcism was a way of destroying manifestations of sexuality which offended the established order. Today, this is most evident in the efforts of some Christians to cast out the 'demon of homosexuality'.

Origen continues his attack on the Delphic oracle by saying that no truly divinely inspired individual would fall into a frenzy, but that their closeness to God would make them exceptionally clear-headed and perceptive:

> If, then, the Pythian priestess is beside herself when she prophesies, what spirit must that be which fills her mind and clouds her judgment with darkness, unless it be of the same order with those demons which many Christians cast out of persons possessed with them? And this, we may observe, they do without the use of any curious acts of magic, or incantations, but merely by prayer and simple adjurations which the plainest person can use.' (2)

So it was that, as one religion fought to supersede another, desperate efforts were made to paint the possessing deity of yore as a devil – one which the new religion could destroy through the power of exorcism.

The Delphic oracle did not take such attacks sitting down. In reply to a man who asked how he might recall his wife from Christianity, the oracle reportedly remarked: 'Let her remain as she pleases in her foolish deception, and sing false laments to her dead God, who was condemned by right-minded judges and punished ignominiously by a violent death.' (3)

The oracle at Delphi was not the only form of trance

mediumship known to the ancient Greeks. On a vastly less grand scale were the so-called 'belly talkers' who, from the little that is known about them, seem to have been women who forecast the future in market-places, perhaps a little like today's gipsy fortune tellers. The belly talkers pronounced their prophecies when in a seeming trance-state, and earned their name from the strange voices with which they spoke. It was believed that this second voice inside the belly talkers belonged to a demon.

Mediumship has remained the domain of women in its modern revival. In ancient times the trance mediums were believed to talk to gods – or demons. Modern mediums, however, seek contact with the dead through falling into a trance and being taken over by a spirit control. It was through the antics of two young girls that spiritualism, as the movement is known, got underway.

On the evening of March 31, 1848, so the story goes, Margaret and Katherine Fox, both in their early teens, began to communicate with a spirit. For some time, the family had heard strange rapping noises in their home, an isolated farmhouse near the town of Arcadia in Wayne Country, New York State. On that particular evening, the girls asked whatever was making the noise to repeat the sounds they made by snapping their fingers. It did so. The sisters soon worked out a rapping system by which the spirit could answer their questions and they were told that the spirit was that of a pedlar who had been murdered in the house and buried in the cellar some years earlier. Within two years the Fox sisters and their mother had become successful mediums and before long, countless people throughout New York State were attempting to communicate with the dead.

The craze soon swept America and crossed to Europe, reaching England in 1852.

By the mid 1850s, Kate Fox was being paid more than a thousand dollars a year by an American businessman in return for agreeing to give free seances to all genuine investigators. In 1888 the sisters confessed that their mediumship had been a fraud. Kate Fox was arrested for drunkenness and idleness in New York. She died an alcoholic in 1892 and her sister died the following year. Despite the many scandals and accusations of fraud which plagued spiritualism, the movement flourished.

One of England's most famous mediums, Florence Cook, was constantly plagued by a spirit calling itself the Devil. Born in 1856 in Hackney, London, Florence was a small, dark and pretty girl, the daughter of a printer. In her mid-teens she began to fall into trances. This was a fairly common experience for young mediums – and the first approaches of the spirits themselves were not always pleasant.

Florence began to attend meetings of the Dalston Spiritualists' Association where she underwent a type of training in order that she would be able to control her spirit guides. It was generally understood that unless novice mediums underwent this training, they would be deranged by the spirits rather than possessed by them. Florence's mediumistic powers developed quickly. Before long she began to experiment with materializations, at first succeeding only in producing a 'death-like face, with staring eyes' (4). Later, however, she managed to materialize 'Katie King', who became Florence's regular spirit control and would appear before the gathered spiritualists while Florence allegedly remained bound in a cupboard.

According to a newspaper report of one of Florence's

sessions, the young woman, dressed in black, was tied to a chair in a corner cupboard, where supposedly the darkness and seclusion enabled her to pass into a trance and so allow the spirit called Katie King to enter her.

While the sitters sang spiritualist songs, 'a tall female figure [Katie King] draped classically in white, with bare arms and feet, did enter at the open door . . . and stood statue-like before us, spoke a few words, and retired; after which we . . . found pretty Miss B. (Miss Blank, Florence Cook) with her dress as before, knots and seals secure, and her boots on!' (5) To prevent accusations of fraud, Florence's wrists would be tied with tape, the knot sealed with wax and the ends of the tape tied to a chair outside the cabinet. Her spirit guide, Katie King, was even photographed on occasions. Florence was, however, caught out in 1880 when two young men grabbed hold of Katie King, only to find that it was Florence herself. Despite this, many spiritualists continued to believe in her powers.

Not all spirit controls were as attractive as Katie King, with her long auburn hair falling in ringlets down her white robes. 'Lenore', the spirit control of one of Florence's friends, apparently smelt like a putrid corpse, as if she had been buried a few weeks and dug up again.

In her heyday, Florence was paid a stipend by a Manchester businessman, but she died aged forty-eight virtually penniless. Her husband, whom she had married several years prior to her death, had forbidden her to continue as a medium and it was only when she fell ill that he allowed her to take up her work once again. Although she made an immediate recovery, a younger generation of mediums was now grabbing the limelight.

By this time, moreover, Florence had begun to complain

of bad experiences with unpleasant spirits and her family's home was subjected to the antics of an unfriendly poltergeist.

Although spiritualism from its early days attracted droves of Christians, many consider that the Bible specifically bans believers from mediumship. According to the Authorised Version of the Bible, Deuteronomy, Chapter 18, Verses 10–11: 'There shall not be found among you,' anyone who is 'a consulter with familiar spirits' – a description which is translated as a 'medium' in the New International Version and Revised Standard Version of the Bible.

Florence was not the only medium to be troubled by less than pleasant experiences. Elizabeth d'Esperance was not at all taken with the sensation of being possessed by some other being:

'It is a horrible feeling, thus losing hold of one's identity,' she wrote in her autobiography, *Shadow Land*. 'I long to put out one of these hands that are lying so helplessly, and touch someone just to know if I am myself or only a dream – if "Anna" [her spirit control] be I, or I am lost as it were, in her identity . . . How long will there be two of us? Which will it be in the end? Shall I be "Anna" or "Anna" be I?' (6)

At times, Elizabeth was even persuaded that her facility for being taken over by spirit beings was the work of the Devil.

Women were judged to be particularly skilled mediums because of their supposedly inherent passivity and lack of intelligence – as well as their lack of education. It was this passivity which was believed to enable the spirit beings to enter and to possess them.

But in Victorian England, women's supposed facility for being possessed also gave them a degree of power. For a start, for those who became professional mediums, it provided a source of income. Other women became professional speakers – but it was allegedly the spirits who spoke, not the women themselves. Once again, this could be seen as enabling the woman speaker to avoid personal responsibility – an accusation time and again levelled against those claiming to be possessed. But though this accusation certainly has a degree of truth in it, the women were none the less up there, holding centre stage, and lecturing to their audiences on issues such as social conditions and women's liberation – as well as spirituality. There is, moreover, no denying the power and influence of twentieth-century women mediums such as the late Doris Stokes who could pack out halls with thousands of men and women who believed her every utterance.

Possession as a means to liberation has not been confined to Western women. In some sectors of the Islamic world it is considered fashionable for a woman to be taken over by a so-called 'zar' spirit. Zar spirits are particularly active in Egypt, Ethiopia, the Sudan and at Mecca, Islam's holy city. The spirits cause the woman to suffer from a type of melancholic sickness and when she is in their possession she is freed from responsibility for her actions and may smoke and drink to her heart's content.

One account of the zar phenomenon describes how whereas men are likely to call in a doctor or religious leader when faced with a case of zar possession, the women always insist on turning for help to one of a number of old women known as exorcists. The old woman will often talk with the zar spirit as though she were conducting a normal conversation, although sometimes she will speak in a special zar language, which no man can understand without the old woman interpreting for him. The zar spirit will almost inevitably tell the old woman that he is quite willing to leave the possessed woman on a particular date, provided that certain ceremonies are performed and demands fulfilled.

Generally, the demands take the form of requests for beautiful new clothes and jewellery. Naturally, since the zar spirit manifests itself in the possessed woman, it is she who receives the gifts.

On the day specified for the zar ceremony, the possessed woman's friends and relatives gather in her home for a party with food and drink, and perhaps some light entertainment such as flute-playing. The possessed woman dresses up in her new finery and the exorcist's assistants play a specific rhythm on their drums, to which the possessed woman sways and dances. The dancing, interspersed with partying, can last for several days. At the climax of the ceremony the possessed woman faints, at which point the exorcist declares her free of the zar spirit.

Sometimes the zar ceremony is less civilized. During the drumming, the women guests might also become possessed by the zar spirit. Their features become noticeably altered, they beat themselves, bang their heads against the walls, weep, howl and attempt to strangle themselves. Only when they are given a particular gift – such as a silver ring – will they return to their normal composure.

In Victorian England, automatic writing helped some women achieve purely practical ends. The woman would sit holding a pen to a sheet of blank paper and wait for the spirit to possess her and guide her hand over the paper. Most of the messages either concerned the minutiae of everyday life or were of the spiritually uplifting and morally exemplary variety.

Sometimes, however, the possessing spirit would leave the woman and she would look down at the piece of paper to find that she had, for instance, been told to leave her husband. But much more important than this was the fact that automatic writing was a way in which women could 'get away' with giving vent to supposedly unwomanly emotions. Sometimes the woman would look down at the sheet of paper after the spirit had departed and discover a screed of obscenities and improprieties.

In such cases, the women tended immediately to consider themselves to have been possessed by an evil spirit. But this ability for women to give vent to a repressed side of their natures while denying all responsibility for the manifestation was almost certainly a cathartic experience.

It was this licence to give vent to pent-up sexual emotions which is believed to have been at the root of one of the most famous ever cases of alleged spirit possession – that of the nuns of Loudun. The outbreak occurred in the seventeenth century and received a fresh bout of interest following Aldous Huxley's examination of the events in his 1952 book *The Devils of Loudun* and Ken Russell's 1971 film *The Devils*.

In 1617 Urbain Grandier was appointed parish priest of Saint Pierre du Marche in the town of Loudun, Poitiers. The handsome, elegant and wealthy priest immediately caused a flutter among the townspeople and rumours of his having affairs with some of the most well-connected women abounded. In 1630 Grandier's lifestyle caught up with him and he was arrested for and found guilty of immorality. Being well-connected, the setback proved only temporary and within a year he was restored to his former position. But

Grandier's success with women and seemingly charmed life had by now won him many enemies, some of whom approached Father Mignon, confessor to a convent of Ursuline nuns.

One of Father Mignon's young relatives was suspected of having a child by Grandier. It was not difficult, therefore, for Grandier's enemies to persuade Father Mignon to help them take their revenge. The plan was soon hatched: Father Mignon would persuade some of the nuns in his care to feign possession, and to claim that Grandier had bewitched them. The Mother Superior, Jeanne des Anges, and another nun happily went along with the plan. At the drop of a hat, they would fall into fits and speak in hoarse, barely recognizable, voices.

Jeanne des Anges appears to have been a strange woman. The daughter of a baron, she had delighted in the luxuries of life before becoming a nun, whereupon she was transformed into a humble, and devoutly pious woman. She claimed that Grandier would appear to her in dreams, not as a parish priest but as a radiant, gloriously bedecked angel. When the apparition spoke, however, it was with the voice of a devil – one who would, apparently, encourage her to indulge in wild sexual acts. Jeanne purported to fight against the temptation by beating herself and subjecting herself to stringent penances. Soon, the convent rang to the sound of her shrieks and ravings and gradually other nuns, too, were subjected to the strange dreams. What began as a deliberate deception seems to have become self-perpetuating.

The situation was ripe for exploitation and Father Mignon, aided by Father Pierre Barre, did not hesitate to milk it for all it was worth. Together, the two priests set about exorcizing the shrieking nuns who fell about in fits and threw themselves into remarkable contortions. Jeanne finally came up with an explanation for her behaviour: she was possessed by two demons, Asmodeus and Zabulon, who had found their way into her via a bunch of roses which had allegedly been sent by Father Grandier and thrown over the convent wall.

Grandier quickly realized the danger he was in and asked that the allegedly possessed nuns be isolated. His request was forwarded to the convent, but ignored. He then wrote to the Archbishop of Bordeaux requesting help. The archbishop sent his doctor to examine the nuns. Despite a thorough examination, the doctor could find no evidence of possession and the archbishop put an end to the exorcisms and instructed the nuns to be confined in their cells.

For a while, a semblance of normality returned to the convent. But Grandier's enemies were not defeated. One of Jeanne's relatives, Jean de Laubardemont, told his friend Cardinal Richelieu of the strange goings-on at the convent and the cardinal appointed him head of a commission the aim of which was to get Grandier convicted as a witch. The exorcisms began again. This time they were conducted in public and led by one Father Tranquille, together with Father Surin.

The tide was definitely turning strongly against Grandier. At this point, several of his former mistresses confessed to having had affairs with him. The stories they told were far from being straightforward tales of impropriety. Instead, they abounded with claims of incest, of sacrilege and of sexual cavortings having taken place in the inner sanctums of the church. Moreover, by now the nuns were having even more explicit dreams and hallucinations which were adjudged to provide yet further proof of Grandier being at the very least an agent of the Devil. Another demon was dredged up by Jeanne, who claimed it was Isacaaron, the demon of debauchery. She even claimed she had been impregnated by the Devil and went through a phantom pregnancy. According to her own account:

> My mind was often filled with blasphemies and sometimes I uttered them without being able to take any thought to stop myself. I felt for God a continual aversion and nothing inspired me with greater hatred than the spectacle of His goodness . . . for the demon beclouded me in such a way that I hardly distinguished his desires from mine; he gave me, moreover, a strong aversion for my religious calling, so that sometimes when he was in my head I tore all my veils and such of my sisters' as I could lay hands on; I trampled them underfoot, I chewed them, cursing the hour when I took the vows. (7)

At the end of his tether, Grandier finally determined to exorcize the nuns himself. Not surprisingly, he failed.

The so-called evidence against Grandier continued to mount. It included a written pact between Grandier and the Devil, which was supposedly signed by Grandier along with numerous demons. The pact also included a message written by the demon Asmodeus. Interestingly enough, it was in the handwriting of Jeanne.

In November 1633, Grandier was thrown into prison at the castle of Angers and the 'Devil's Mark' was found on him. According to medieval witch-hunters, anyone who had pledged themselves to the Devil would be marked in a secret place, for instance under the eyelid or inside the body. Such marks were easily discovered – very often they were birthmarks – and in Grandier's case this proved no exception. The doctor and apothecary attending Grandier insisted that there were no such marks, but no one paid any attention to them.

As it began to hit home what was likely to happen to Grandier, several nuns began to retract their accusations. But Richelieu's henchman, Laubardemont, was not going to let anything stand in his way. Even Jeanne des Anges finally seems to have come to her senses. When she appeared in court, she placed a noose around her neck and threatened to hang herself if her retraction of all her previous accusations was not accepted. Her efforts proved useless. Many of those who sought to defend Grandier were themselves accused of witchcraft and had to flee from France.

In August 1634 Grandier was sentenced: he was to be subjected to every known torture and then burned alive. Even under the most horrific torture, Grandier refused to confess to his supposed crimes. Father Tranquille was so frustrated that he ordered both Grandier's legs to be broken and claimed that every time the priest prayed to God he was really praying to the Devil. Some took pity on Grandier and promised to allow him to make a final statement before being killed, but on his way to the stake he was drenched with holy water which choked him thereby preventing him from speaking. His sympathizers had also promised to strangle him before he was burnt, but the garrotte had been specially knotted in order that it could not be tightened.

Almost all the priests who had carried out the exorcisms came to sticky ends. One died within a month – a death that had been foretold by Grandier with his last gasp. Father Tranquille went mad and died within five years; another priest was banished from the Church for accusing a priest of rape. Father Surin became so haunted by the exorcisms that he became almost totally incapacitated, unable to feed or dress himself and constantly plagued by terrifying visions. In May 1635, Surin wrote to a friend:

Things have gone so far that God has permitted, I think for my sins, what has perhaps never been seen in the Church, that in the exercise of my ministry the devil passes out of the body of the possessed woman and entering into mine assaults and confounds me, agitates and troubles me visibly, possessing me for several hours like a demoniac. I cannot explain to you what happens within me during that time and how this spirit unites with mine without depriving me either of consciousness or liberty of soul, nevertheless making himself like another me and as if I had two souls, one of which is dispossessed of its body and the use of its organs and stands aside watching the actions of the other which has entered into them . . . When I desire by the motion of one of these two souls to make the sign of the cross on my mouth, the other averts my hand with great swiftness and grips my finger in its teeth to bite me with rage. (8)

With the help of another priest, Surin finally recovered.

Despite the horror of Grandier's ending, and despite the many retractions, the antics of the nuns of Loudun continued. Sightseers flocked to the convent to watch the nuns lifting up their skirts and muttering all kinds of obscenities. Some would beat themselves, bend themselves backwards into hoops or walk on their hands. Three years after Grandier's death the show was stopped by Cardinal

Richelieu whose niece convinced him that the whole affair had been a set-up.

For many onlookers, the spectacular exorcism shows at Loudun demonstrated the power of the Catholic Church over that of the Church of England. What becomes clear is that, throughout history, both possession and exorcism have been used as tools of power and propaganda – sometimes a covert means by which women could gather power to themselves, sometimes as a method of settling scores within a community, and sometimes on a broader and more overt scale, to demonstrate the superior power of a particular religion or denomination.

In the late sixteenth century the exorcisms conducted by Puritan preacher John Darrell were used as propaganda by the Puritans. As one of John Darrell's supporters said:

'. . . if the Church of England have this power to cast out devils, then the Church of Rome is a false Church; for there can be but one true Church, the principal mark whereof (as they say) is to work miracles, and of them this is the greatest, namely to cast out devils.' (9)

As far as many leading figures within the Church of England were concerned, however, Darrell was nothing more than a fraud. He was convicted as such in May 1599 after having, so he claimed, exorcized the Devil from William Sommers of Nottingham. Sommers was a young man who suffered fits and would indulge in obscene behaviour – including bestiality – in front of onlookers. When Darrell exorcized him, Sommers named several witches he claimed were responsible for his condition and Darrell had them arrested. Eventually, Sommers claimed to have faked his fits, and even gave a detailed account of how

Darrell had helped him to refine his performance. The whole furore resulted in the ruling in Canon 72 of the new Church Canons of 1604 that, 'No minister or ministers shall . . . without the license or direction of the Bishop . . . attempt upon any pretence whatsoever either of possession or obsession, by fasting or prayer, to cast out any devil or devils, under pain of the imputation of imposture or cozenage, and deposition from the ministry.'

The temptation to use possession and exorcism as propaganda for the Christian cause must be enormous. And, though time and again exorcists insist that their ministry by no means rests on their own personal power but on the power of Christ, they are inevitably endowed with power by their followers. To avoid allowing such power to go to one's head must prove a difficult challenge.

According to Pentecostal pastor and exorcist, Graham Baldwin, 'There are some people in the Church who use the deliverance ministry as a form of control. They will tell someone,'If you come and stay with me for a month I will deal with your demon.' People who do that are obviously getting some kind of buzz, some sense of self-worth by directing people's lives.'

In Britain today, Peter Horrobin, the founder and leader of Christian healing centre Ellel Grange, near Lancaster, has developed an ardent following. Some 7,000 people have received personal ministry from members of the Ellel Grange team, and about 20,000 have attended courses and conferences held there. Detractors have rechristened Horrobin's centre 'Hellhell' Grange, an appropriate name, they believe, for a place which lays so much emphasis on the Devil and his works.

Like many other exorcists, Horrobin believes he has a

gift of discernment, that he simply KNOWS whether or not someone has a demon. In his opinion, we are currently witnessing a 'generation of demonized people'. If we take a look at how Horrobin believes a person can become demonized, his statement is not so surprising. He claims, for instance, that many people are demonized with sexual spirits through watching television. Then there are those people whose speech systems are apparently in good working order, but who are nevertheless dumb. According to Horrobin, 'a significant proportion of those . . . are as they are because of the presence of a controlling demon.' There again, could Horrobin simply be prescribing as demonic something which is not yet medically understood?

Even more worrying, Horrobin recounts how relatives of the football fans who died at Hillsborough watched the disaster on live television and then asks: 'I wonder how many of these people have actually been demonized through the shock of seeing those pictures in their own home and are in need of deliverance as well as medical care?' And Horrobin does not see demons as some vague product of a troubled soul but as very real, though disembodied, creatures with a mind, will and personality of their own.

These creatures often crop up, he claims, in the area of sexual activity: 'Where there has been sexual sin . . . of any nature, deliverance is usually an important part of the healing process. This is especially so in the case of women who have been taken advantage of by men, *whether or not the sexual participation was voluntary . . . or involuntary in the case of those who have been forcibly abused, either as children or as adults.*' (my italics) Horrobin then goes on to say that 'as many as one in two of the women who have come to us for help have been sexually abused at some time during their life. Most have also been demonized as a result . . .' (10)

One Christian minister tells of having been sought out by several distressed women after Horrobin had 'discerned' they were sexually abused when children and that as a result they had become infested by demons.

Horrobin also believes that homesickness can be a sign of demonization. So someone staying at Ellel Grange who wishes to return home is possibly demonized?

An exorcist's power of suggestion can be tremendous, as a tale related in a British newspaper in 1992 illustrates. A woman had appeared on television claiming she had been forced to kill her own baby during a devil worship ceremony. Afterwards, she told the newspaper her story. The woman, Louise, had been living with her two children and husband in Staffordshire. The marriage was unhappy and a Christian evangelist suggested Louise should visit Ellel Grange. Before going there, Louise had been seeing a psychiatrist.

'I had been ill and felt suicidal. At one stage I begged to be admitted to a mental hospital. Then I became a born-again Christian and people at my church paid for me and my husband to go to Ellel Grange. There, the charismatics had an overpowering effect on me. In many ways it was the worst three months of my life. They told me I was possessed by demons because of the sins of my mother and father. They prayed over me in tongues and taught me to face my own guilt.'

Horrobin then told Louise that one of his helpers had experienced a vision. According to Louise:

'He said he had seen a mind-picture of me standing over a tiny baby, helping a devil priest to wield a knife. We cut into the baby's chest and the blood was collected and we drank it. The baby's body was a sacrifice to Satan.'

Up until then, Louise had been totally unaware of having given birth to this baby.

'I screamed and pleaded with them to please stop saying it. I had a sort of fit, and had to be held down. I fought people off physically. Finally I broke down and confessed it was true. I said "Yes, I did it. I killed my own little daughter and helped others to kill their babies." ' (11)

Louise is still convinced that she killed this child.

Ellel Grange has produced a video about the work carried on there. A type of promotional–cum–information pack, it includes scenes of an exorcism. In 1991, a United States television network broadcast the exorcism of a sixteen–year–old girl from Florida who had been hospitalized for psychotic behaviour. The report lasted almost half an hour. Ominous music played in the background as the young woman, strapped to a chair, barked and gabbled. The exorcist, a Roman Catholic priest, pressed a cross to her face and recited the rite of exorcism. Afterwards, the priests sent her home but she was re-admitted to hospital within a few days and given antipsychotic drugs before being released. The priests involved in the case claimed that the coverage would offer 'hope to those who may be afflicted'.

Others are not so sure. They feel the programme trivialized the whole issue of evil. And they say that by concentrating on evil as a devil which can be cast out of individuals, we ignore the evils apparent in society such as poverty and oppression.

It is a problem which time and again confronts those in the field of exorcism. While seeking to emphasize the very real threat presented by the demonic, they realize that in doing so they risk inoculating people against it so that they come to dismiss its reality. This must, say exorcists, be the cleverest lie of the Devil.

An equal but opposite problem is that, by emphasizing the power of the Devil, he is given too much credibility. According to exorcist and Baptist minister Nigel Wright: 'to believe in God means that we radically disbelieve in the power of darkness. This does not mean that we think it is an illusion. We are mindful of its reality. But belief in God means that we reject the power of darkness.'

None the less, there is no sign that the fervour with which New Christians sing out from the rooftops about the Devil is going to abate. Indeed, as the year 2000 approaches, it is likely to increase, and with it the number of exorcisms. The approach of the millennium brings with it a sense that the world is going to experience change on a cosmic scale. Many Christians take this to signify that we are currently in the 'last days', a time during which our battle with the Devil must take on a renewed vigour.

Attempts by the mainstream denominations to regulate exorcism provide some degree of control and accountability. The charismatic and house church movements are, however, the fastest-growing branches of Christianity in Britain today. With their increasing emphasis on the supernatural power of God, and almost inevitably, simultaneous decrease in emphasis on the authority of the Established Church hierarchies, exorcisms along the lines of those conducted by Peter Horrobin are likely to flourish. Perhaps the final irony is that exorcists such as this are helping to elevate Satan to the status of God.

References

CHAPTER 1

1   *Daily Mail* 28 October 1974
2   *The Times*
3   Trevor Dearing, *Exit the Devil* (Logos Publishing International Ltd, England 1976) p. 99
4   Michael Harper, *Spiritual Warfare* (1970; Servant Books, Ann Arbor, Michigan rev. ed. 1984) p. 5
5   David Watson, *Hidden Warfare* (Kingsway Publications Ltd, Eastbourne 1983) p. 45
6   Rudolf Bultmann in H. W. Bartsch (ed), *Kerygma and Myth* (London 1953) p. 5
7   Peter Anderson, *Satan's Snare* (Evangelical Press, Hertfordshire 1988) p. 29

CHAPTER 2

1   Chris Bray, *The Occult Census: Statistical Analyses and Results* (Sorcerer's Apprentice, Leeds 1989) pp. 3, 5
2   Selwyn Hughes, *The Christian Counsellor* Vol 2 Number 2 'The Demonic in Counselling' (Part 2)
3   Hal Lindsey, *Combat Faith* (Bantam Books, New York 1986) p. 164
4   Merrill Unger, *Demons in the World Today* (Tyndale, Wheaton 1971)
5   *The Magazine of the ICCC* (International Christian

Chamber of Commerce) May 1991 Issue 12, p. 3

6   Jessie Penn-Lewis, *The Spiritual Warfare* (Overcomer Publications, Poole, Dorset n.d.) p. 6

7   John White, *The Flight* (InterVarsity Press, Downers Grove, Illinois 1976) p. 216

8   Luke Chapter 8 v.31

9   Mark Chapter 5 v.10

CHAPTER 3

1   Russ Parker, *The Occult: Deliverance from Evil* (InterVarsity Press, Leicester 1989) p. 15

2   Roger Ellis, *The Occult and Young People* (Kingsway Publications, Eastbourne 1989) p. 70

3   *Doorways to Danger* (Evangelical Alliance, London 1987)

4   *Daily Mail* 13 March 1990

5   Selwyn Hughes, *The Christian Counsellor* Vol 2 Number 2 'The Demonic in Counselling' (Part 2)

6   Harnack, *Die Mission*, vol. i. p. 141. Cited in T. K. Oesterreich, *Possession* (Citadel Press, New Jersey 1974) p. 164

7   Like Chapter 10 vv 19–20

8   Cited Oesterreich p. 165

9   Flavius Josephus, *Antiquities of the Jews*, book viii, chap ii

10   Testament of Solomon 15:14

11   Cited in Graham Twelftree, *Christ Triumphant* (Hodder and Stoughton, London 1985) p. 40

12   ibid

13   ibid p. 40

14   Russ Parker p. 30

CHAPTER 4

1   See Dom Robert Petitpierre (ed), *Exorcism* (SPCK, London 1972) p. 45
2   Don Cupitt, *Exorcism* (SCM, London 1979) pp. 50–51
3   Report of Proceedings of the General Synod Vol 6 No 2 (July 1975) p. 361
4   The *Guardian* 3 May 1985
5   Luke Chapter 10 v.19

CHAPTER 5

1   Michael Perry (ed), *Deliverance* (SPCK, London 1987) p. 28
2   Cited Keith Thomas, *Religion and the Decline of Magic* (1971. Penguin, London, 1991) p. 710

CHAPTER 6

1   Cited in Jeanne Achterberg, *Woman as Healer* (Rider, London, 1990) p. 72. Arnald of Villanova, *Antidotarum*, cap. 3 (from edition of his complete works, published in Lyons, France, 1532)
2   Keith Thomas, p. 32
3   ibid p. 211
4   ibid pp. 211–12
5   Luke Chapter 13, v.32
6   Luke Chapter 9, v.1
7   Ernaldus, *Vita Bernardi Abbatis Claravellensis*, cap. III pars 13–15 in Migne, *Patrologioe Cursus completus*, vol. clxxxv pp. 276 sq. Also *Acta Sanctorum*, Augusti, vol. iv, p. 282. Cited in Oesterreich p. 179

8 Gorres, *Die Christliche Mystik*, Regensburg, 1842, vol. iv, part i, p. 332, from the Acta Sanctorum, Jun 6, c.viii, p. 834

9 The lives of St Francis of Assisi, by Thomas of Celano, trans. by A. G. Ferrers Howell, London, 1908 p. 66. Cited in Oesterreich p. 181

10 *Histoire des Diables de Loudun*, Amsterdam, 1716, pp. 226 sq. Cited in Oesterreich p. 18

11 J. Kerner, *Geschichten Besessener Neuerer Zeit*, Stuttgart, 1834 p. 122. Cited Oesterreich p. 122

12 Keith Thomas, pp. 249–50

13 Rudolf Bultmann in H. W. Bartsch (ed), *Kerygma and Myth* (SPCK, London, 1953)

14 Cited Alex Owen, *The Darkened Room* (Virago Press, London, 1989) p. 142

15 Cited Oesterreich pp. 126–7

16 Dr L. S. Forbes Winslow, *Spiritualist Madness* Bailliere, Tindall & Cox, London, 1877) p. 2. Cited Alex Owen, p. 147

17 *Diagnostic and Statistical Manual of Mental Disorders* (1980) American Psychiatric Association p. 257

18 Robert Phillips, introduction to Truddi Chase, *When Rabbit Howls* (Jove Books, New York 1990) p. 10

19 Bennett, G. Braun, MD, 'Issues in the Psychotherapy of Multiple Personality Disorder' in *Treatment of Multiple Personality Disorder* ed by Bennett G. Braun (American Psychiatric Press, Washington 1986) p. 21

20 James G. Friesen, *Uncovering the Mystery of MPD* (Here's Life Publishers, California 1991) p. 231

21 ibid pp. 222–3

22 Jerry Savelle, *God's Provision for Healing* (Tulsa: Harrison House) p. 8

23 Kenneth Copeland, *Welcome To the Family. A Guide to Salvation, the Baptism of the Holy Spirit and Healing* (KCP Publications, Fort Worth, Texas 1979 reprinted 1990) pp. 27–8

24 *Seattle Times*, 19 October 1988. Cited in Eileen Barker *New Religious Movements*, (HMSO, London 1989) p. 62

CHAPTER 7

1 E. Curtius, *Griechische Geschichte* (Berlin, 1887) vol i, p. 549. Cited Oesterreich p. 324

2 Origen, *Contra Celsum*, bk. vii chaps iii–iv

3 Augustine De Civitate Dei, xix, 23

4 *The Spiritualist*, 12 December 1873 p. 451

5 *Daily Telegraph*, 12 August 1873. Cited Alex Owen p. 48

6 Elizabeth d'Esperance, *Shadow Land* (Redway, London 1897) pp. 345–7

7 Soeur Jeanne des Anges, 'Bibliotheque diabolique', p. 71. Cited Oesterreich, p. 50

8 *Cruels effets de la vengeance du Cardinal Richelieu ou Histoire des Diables de Loudun*. Cited Oesterreich, p. 51

9 George More, *A True Discourse Concerning the Certaine Possession and Dispossession of 7 Person in one familie in Lancashire* (1600) p. 5. Cited in Keith Thomas p. 577

10 Peter Horrobin, *Healing through Deliverance* (Sovereign World Ltd, Chichester 1991)

11 The *Mail on Sunday*, 1 March 1992